D0559919

VISIONARY SELLING

HOW TO GET TO TOP EXECUTIVES—
AND HOW TO SELL THEM
WHEN YOU'RE THERE

Barbara Geraghty

SIMON & SCHUSTER

SIMON & SCHUSTER
Rockefeller Center
1230 Avenue of the Americas
New York, NY 10020

Designed by Irving Perkins Associates

Manufactured in the United States of America

3 5 7 9 10 8 6 4 2

Library of Congress Cataloging-in-Publication Data
Geraghty, Barbara, date.
Visionary selling : how to get to top executives—and how to sell them when you're there / Barbara Geraghty.
p. cm.
Includes bibliographical references and index.
1. Selling. 2. Selling—Key accounts. 3. Executives. I. Title.
HF5438.25.G47 1998 97-23935
658.85—dc21 CIP

ISBN 0-684-83985-7

Acknowledgments

The ideas and concepts in this book were formulated after numerous interviews and appointments with top executives and sales managers at corporations across America. They convinced me of the need for a new paradigm of selling skills to confront and capitalize on the business realities of the 1990s. Their generous investment of time and valuable input are greatly appreciated.

I am also grateful to my friends and peers at National Speakers Association, who provided enthusiastic encouragement and helpful critiques of the material. Special thanks to Michael Larsen–Elizabeth Pomada Literary Agents and Frederic Hills, Hilary Black, and Burton Beals at Simon & Schuster.

Many thanks to the following corporate contributors who took time from their schedules to provide input:

Peter Allocca, Exide Electronics
George Bennett, ATC Communications
Keith Goodwin, Hewlett-Packard
Michael D. Newman, 3M
Richard Normington, Pacific Bell
Jerome Oleshansky, Owens Corning
Robert Peebler, Landmark Graphics
Leo Rivera, Silicon Graphics
James Sheehy, Landmark Graphics
Volney Spaulding, Silicon Graphics
Chris Turner, Xerox Business Services
Jon Wampler, PacifiCare
Morley Winograd, AT&T

To my husband, Colin,
who understands my vision, eases my frustration,
and shares my joy

Contents

Introduction

I am a keynote speaker specializing in advanced, leading edge sales skills for major account salespeople. My personal sales career spans thirteen years. I am not like some sales speakers who do not sell. To quote my personal hero, Scott Adams of *Dilbert* fame, "That is like writing a firsthand account of the Donner party based on the fact that you once ate beef jerky. Me, I've gnawed an ankle or two." I've spent the last thirteen years gnawing on ankles: selling to top executives and interviewing top executives. I've researched and observed what makes them tick, how they think, what intrigues them, and how we can add value at this level. I continue to perform the majority of the selling activities for my business, because I love sales and I am passionate about selling. When I am down and need a lift, I make a few cold calls. I cannot imagine my life without daily sales activities.

In the Beginning . . .

It wasn't always this way. My initial venture into sales was pure serendipity, born of desperation. I was a thirty-year-old single mother who had just finished college. Three years of full-time college and part-time work, with two young children to support, had left me financially destitute. Holes in the radiator of my car, holes in the roof of my house. You get the picture.

As an advertising major in college, I'd studied the very successful advertising campaign of an upstart rival to AT&T called MCI. Driving down the freeway one day, I spotted the MCI building.

On impulse I went into the lobby and inquired about employment. I was led directly into an office. This is good, I thought. When I told the man behind the desk that I was interested in working in their advertising department, however, he laughed out loud. Their advertising was handled by a big firm in New York, he said, and decisions were made from corporate headquarters in Washington, D.C. But would I be interested in a job in telemarketing sales?

My reaction, looking back, was revealing. Telemarketing sales was one step above fast-food server, in my opinion. But I was desperate, so I accidentally embarked on a fabulous career . . . a career that was always challenging, sometimes fascinating, and led to a thorough knowledge of business, a wealth of influential contacts, and unbelievable financial rewards.

My career in corporate sales, from telemarketer to top sales manager at Sprint, spanned a decade. Looking back on my sales performance, I realize that I never sold the way most people did at the time. I was focused on building relationships when most salespeople were intent on maintaining control of the appointment. I began selling higher in the organization because I didn't have the patience to sell to "technical buyer" types who require an avalanche of information and detail, and still cannot make a decision. I am a perfect fit for "prove the value and results, and you've got my business" types. I don't care if they hold my feet to the fire. I'm used to it; my feet have been sizzling since 1983.

My Work Today

In my work with corporations today, I am hired by vice presidents of sales. When I ask them how their people need to perform better or differently, they tell me that the 90s require a new culture of selling, with a different skill set. Technical presentations are out, and value creation is in. I hear this statement over and over:

"Our people are doing a better job of getting to a higher-level decision maker, but once they get there, they don't know what to say."

Three essential components of selling to top executives will be covered in this book:

- Building confidence to approach top executives
- Understanding how to capture their attention and gain access
- Knowing what to say when you get there.

An Analogy Between Visionary Selling and a Job Search

As I developed Visionary Selling, some salespeople I spoke with were having a hard time understanding the concept. Then I had a discussion with an executive who works with individuals on career planning. "That is the exact process required to successfully complete a high-level job search," she said. "You must discover new ways to open doors and capture attention. You must conduct ferocious research to learn as much as possible about the company. And once you get there, you'd better blow their socks off so they see the tremendous value you can offer their company."

In counseling her clients she tells them to abandon all preconceived notions of what it takes to achieve a successful job search, such as the following:

1. My resume is important.
2. I don't know anyone at the company.
3. I have to go through the human resources department.
4. They won't hire me if they don't have a position.
5. They won't consider me because I have no experience in this industry.

I believe these are the same concerns that sabotage many salespeople:

1. My brochure is important.
2. I don't know anyone at the company.
3. I have to go through the purchasing department.
4. They won't buy my product because it isn't in the budget.
5. They won't work with me because I have no experience in their industry.

Visionary Selling requires you to suspend your assumptions about the sales process and open your thinking to new possibilities. You *can* enter a new door by meeting with top executives. You can create value for them and their companies by sharing information and ideas that are intriguing and useful. Stories of people who have done so are on the pages that follow.

What Will You Get out of This?

What is the value of Visionary Selling to your customers?

- Everyone, individually and collectively, in companies wants to be understood.
- It saves them valuable time: They don't need to educate you on their identity.
- It increases your ability to design strategically brilliant proposals and solutions.

What are the benefits to you, the salesperson?

- It differentiates you from other salespeople who are calling on them.
- It provides a strong competitive advantage: Everyone else is selling solutions.
- Decision makers with whom you interact will recognize your comprehension of who they are and what they stand for.

- It cuts to the chase. You're connecting with the heart and soul of the corporation.
- It demonstrates your willingness to "go the extra mile."
- It establishes your credibility as a professional.
- It increases your fulfillment and motivation in your job by raising your performance to a higher level of professional challenge and value.

When to Use Visionary Selling

Visionary Selling is not a new sales gimmick. It is not a quicker, easier, surefire way to sell more. It is not for every salesperson, for every sales situation, or for every prospective customer. It is a high-risk, high-reward selling tool to be used selectively. A significant investment of time is required to complete an intense research process and to formulate a strong value proposition which includes innovative, insightful ideas that a top executive might benefit from.

Visionary Selling is especially applicable in large, complex sales situations where a vision alliance and a solid strategy are essential. Use it for the big ones that require everything you've got and then some, and that will produce significant rewards. The gestation period for a mosquito is twenty-three hours. For an elephant, it is twenty-three months. But when you get it, it's huge. You have to prepare more, work harder, and often wait longer for some sales. But when you get them, they're huge.

If you are ready to ascend to a new tier of selling skills and to progress from sales vendor to business ally, Visionary Selling will show you how.

PART I

A NEW PARADIGM OF SELLING SKILLS

CHAPTER 1

Everything Is Changing . . . Why Not Sales?

What do you need to succeed in sales today? What does it take to surge to the top? What skills are required to perform at the peak of this challenging profession?

You must be intelligent about business and knowledgeable about your industry. You must be masterful at forging relationships and adept at nurturing them. You must be a team leader who can manage all the individuals and departments that serve the customer. And you must be agile and adaptable so you can cope with perpetual change.

But wait, there's more. To succeed in sales today you must penetrate the top executive level of the organization. You must comprehend business principles and financial models. You must understand how top executives think and what they need so you can communicate pertinent information and provocative ideas.

Visionary Selling is a revolutionary sales approach that will challenge your assumptions about how to sell to a corporation. After reading this practical book, you will know how to do the following:

- Target the "C" level of the organization: CEO, CIO, CFO, COO
- Conduct research to discover vision, values, and core competencies
- Identify industry trends and market opportunities

- Package the information into pertinent information and provocative ideas
- Achieve a long-term alliance that transcends today's problems and issues

Changes That Affect the Profession of Sales

Why is this information important now? Visionary Selling responds to change—change in corporate structure and focus, change in technology and its applications, change in demographics and consumer patterns, change that affects the profession of sales.

During the past decade our corporate customers and prospects experienced an astonishing amount of change. They had to undergo the 3 Rs of the 90s: reorganizing, reengineering, and rightsizing. What do these terms and processes really mean? They mean that corporations have accomplished a profound transformation requiring a period of intense business upheaval. Their entire structure has been reconfigured. A flattening of organizations has occurred, with changes in decision-making patterns as a result.

Our Customers Are Anxious and Uncertain

How does this relate to the individuals you sell to? Simple: Every single one of your customers and prospective customers is coping with rapid and unpredictable business change. They are experiencing uncertainty, insecurity, and anxiety. And these feelings are relevant to your business relationship with them.

When I entered the world of sales in 1983, I would begin first appointments with new prospects by asking them about their business. One of my most effective questions was "Where do you see your business headed in the next two years?" I discovered that even prospects who were hesitant to discuss current problems and objectives loved to fantasize about the future.

Go ahead, I dare you. On your next sales call, ask your prospect or customer where he or she sees the business going in the next few years. If your customers are anything like mine, a look of dismay will cross their face as they wonder: "Where will I be in two years? I hardly know where I am today!"

Some acknowledge this bewilderment, while others are in denial. But everyone realizes that the world we live in and do business in will be radically different by the millennium. In the past ten years it seems that everything we have learned has already changed. The world is undergoing a metamorphosis, socially, economically, and technologically. It will continue to affect every single one of us, personally and professionally.

The Evolution of Selling Skills

What does this have to do with selling skills? Think back to when you entered the profession of selling. If it was before 1985, you were probably taught the features and benefits method. Features and benefits. F&B. FAB. This is how it worked: You memorized the features of your product or service and translated them into benefits for your customer. You understood that the customer was uninterested in the technical aspects of what you had to offer and really cared only about "what's in it for me?" The best salespeople discovered exactly what the customer was interested in and then communicated benefits that were selectively based on those interests. Features and benefits selling can be defined by this statement: *This is what* I *have. This is why* you *need it.*

Does features and benefits selling still have value today? Of course—in certain situations and with certain prospects. Let me provide an example. Like many of you, I travel frequently on business. While on the road I end up eating in fast-food restaurants . . . alone. Out of sheer boredom I read anything in sight.

A few months ago I was in a Burger King. Preparing to bite into my Whopper, I was reading the place mat on my tray. It told the history of the Whopper, including the serrated edges on the pickles. Did you know the serrated edges on pickles hold the condiments on the burger? Now this is a real benefit to me. The last thing I want to happen before a big sales appointment is for mayonnaise and mustard to drip down my wrists onto my power suit. I see serrated edges in a new light, and I appreciate Burger King's wisdom for serrating the edges.

The feature? Serrated edges. This is what I have. The benefit? Holds the condiments on burgers. This is what it will do for you. Classic features and benefits selling.

The mid 80s arrived, and a new selling methodology was introduced. This selling tier was called by a variety of names: customer-oriented selling, consultative selling, partnership selling, relationship selling, solutions selling, non-manipulative selling. Call it what you will, the fundamental concept was the same: Put the customer first! And the concept was revolutionary. The focus: resolving the customer's needs or achieving the customer's objectives; establishing a win-win relationship to achieve mutually beneficial solutions; looking upon your customer as a person, not just an order, unit, or commission. This selling method can be defined by the statement: *Here is what* you *need. This is what* I *can do for you.*

A dictionary definition of consultant is "one who gives expert or professional advice." The application of consultative selling skills thrusts the profession of sales to a higher level of integrity and value. As a result of this change in focus, salespeople have learned to ask insightful, probing questions to discover all their customers' needs and objectives, and they listen carefully to detect hidden issues. They may recommend something different from what the customer requested, supporting their proposal with an intelligent rationale for the switch. Occasionally they present a proposal based on information previously unknown to the customer, providing a bold and insightful solution.

Consultative selling is a style that continues to offer value. As long as people have problems, selling solutions will be effective. But with the rapid pace of change in the last ten years, a new tier of selling skills is required. We need a whole new way of thinking about the profession of sales: one that incorporates the change our customers are experiencing as a fundamental maxim of the selling process; one that capitalizes on the gut-wrenching, nerve-jarring apprehension they feel; one that adds value at every level of the corporate organization by providing ideas and information which will enhance the customer's business.

A New Sales Paradigm

It is time for our profession to undergo a radical transformation such as those experienced by manufacturing, management, and technology in the 80s and 90s. We need a new sales paradigm for the twenty-first century.

The mission of Visionary Selling is to offer a compelling new method and valuable tools for aligning with the top executive level in the rapidly changing, technologically advanced corporate world of the millennium. The decade from 1987 to 1997 has been one of the most dynamic in business history. The corporations we sell to have undergone extensive change, and our approach in selling to them must reflect these changes. Our sales tools are stagnant. Why use an old tool to do a new job?

Visionary Selling is an additional tool for your tool pouch. Will you use it all the time? Not necessarily. Sometimes features and benefits selling is adequate. A solution sell is often the perfect approach. Any one of your prospects may require each of the three in a single purchasing decision. By having an additional selling tool in your tool pouch, however, you will be prepared for higher-level, vastly bountiful opportunities as they present themselves.

Unless we proactively update our profession, I predict the profession of sales will experience a decline. To fail to change during a period of intense business upheaval and transformation is to risk becoming irrelevant to a changing world.

Elimination of Middlemen

One of the most startling trends of the last decade has been the elimination of middlemen through the establishment of direct purchasing organizations. Think of Wal-Mart, Price Club, Costco, and Home Depot. The fewer layers between product manufacture and consumer, the lower the price. Consumers have responded favorably to this model and have proven that they are willing to sacrifice some convenience for the benefit of cost savings.

An article in the January 1996 issue of *Sales & Marketing Management* explores a division in the dominant selling paradigm of a direct sales force into low-cost channels or high-end solutions. The article claims that customers are so knowledgeable about certain classes of product that they no longer require the information and service that direct sales representatives provide. "Customers want the product. Period. And they want it at low cost," the article states.

In *The Road Ahead,* Bill Gates, CEO of Microsoft, discusses how the Internet will increase this trend of elimination of distribution. He calls it "friction-free capitalism." It works like this: You want to buy a new stereo. Instead of heading to a local electronics store, you quickly design a little software program to explore the global Net, review the available sources, and order directly from a manufacturer in Taiwan. No need to rely on a middleman, and no need to pay a sales commission. The friction-free economy is one cleared of middlemen and the friction Bill says they cause. The following quote from *The Road Ahead* represents what I consider the sales professional's wake-up call: "The information highway will extend the electronic marketplace and make it the ultimate go-between, the universal middleman. Often the only humans involved in a transaction will be the actual buyer and seller. All the goods for sale in the world will be available for you to examine, compare, and, often, customize."

Salespeople are middlemen! Unless we offer significant value to the customer beyond communication of information, our entire profession is in jeopardy. After all, the Internet communicates features just fine.

One of my clients tells a story of being on a very important customer visit that included executives from both companies. In the middle of the meeting, one of the executives from the customer's company eyed the salesperson and asked, "What are you doing for us to earn your commission?"

How would you answer the question? We must begin to think *now* about how we can make sure that our profession offers value which justifies the commission we receive. As sales professionals we have a choice: be categorized as middlemen who may be replaced to reduce the price of the product or service, or position ourselves in a new way.

In an era when product information and customer support is readily available from many convenient sources, we must increase the value we provide. This peril provides the most exciting challenge we have ever encountered. I suggest that we respond strategically to this threat to our profession.

The Basis of Wealth Has Changed

Consider the changing face of wealth in the world. From the beginning of commerce until 1970, wealth was comprised of material such as land, currency, goods, equipment, inventory, and resources. We have entered the Information Age, and our concept of wealth has evolved. Economists refer to the "triple pillars" of wealth—labor, capital, and raw materials. These have been replaced by *knowledge* as the singular pillar of wealth.

Today, wealth is contained in information and in the application of information to capitalize on opportunities and achieve results. As sales professionals seeking methods to update our profession and increase our value, we recognize the seed of potential in this statement.

To succeed in sales today and tomorrow, we must assist our customers and prospects as they seek new information and the insightful application of that information in order to capitalize on opportunities and achieve results. Otherwise, we will flounder. In business today, anyone who does not contribute to the bottom line is in jeopardy. The corporate world has reported tremendous gains in profitability and even productivity by eliminating numerous layers of personnel. "We are entering an era of organizational change as profound and as pervasive as that caused by the Industrial Revolution," says Lester Thurow, economics professor at MIT's Sloan School of Management. "Companies are organizing themselves in a variety of new ways to make the best use of the resources they have available, both inside and outside the company. Fundamental changes are occurring in the economy that place a special value on knowledge workers, people with special skills who can solve expensive business problems."

Top professional salespeople are knowledge workers with special skills who can solve expensive business problems. In *The Great Crossover: Personal Confidence in the Age of the Microchip,* authors Dan Sullivan, Babs Smith, and Michael Neray assert that the value of simply passing on information will diminish while the value of manipulating information will increase. They refer to three specific skills: filtering (separating the relevant from the unnecessary for specific purposes,) interpreting, and transforming information into new and usable knowledge. Visionary Selling seeks to achieve a leap beyond the filtering of features and benefits selling and the interpreting of solutions selling. The goal is to take ownership of our customers' goals and create value by transforming information into new and usable knowledge for their businesses.

How can we increase the value of professional selling? By implementing a new sales paradigm that focuses on providing value to our customers, which brings them insights and information that will help them capitalize on opportunities and achieve results.

- Visionary Selling requires selling *beyond* the product or service.
- Visionary Selling requires selling *beyond* the solution.
- Visionary Selling connects with concepts such as vision, growth, progress, transformation, and even revolution—and then goes one step beyond.
- Visionary Selling makes a bold and compelling statement:

This is where you *are going. This is how* I *can help you get there.*

CHAPTER 2

Catch Their Vision!

Examine the current environment in corporate America, and several major issues and trends become apparent. Business has become more dynamic and less predictable. Transitions that would have transpired over a decade are now completed in one year. Major technological advances are introduced, integrated, and obsoleted—all within an eighteen-month window of time. Reorganizations are routine. Many managers are responsible for work once performed by several people, resulting in what has been described as the "frayed collar workforce."

Is this a problem or an opportunity for salespeople? Actually, downsizing has created a tremendous opportunity for us. Decision makers are relying on outside sources more than ever before! Due to their increased workload, they are offering us an opportunity to "cross the boundary" of sales and enter their business as an ally.

In one of the top business titles for executive management today, *Competing for the Future,* Gary Hamel and C. K. Prahalad define a new view of strategy that includes "the quest to overcome resource constraints through a creative and unending pursuit of better *resource leverage.*" Companies that intend to be first in the future are leveraging the resource of information and assistance offered by salespeople who serve their company.

Before 1985, salespeople with superior product knowledge were at the top of their field. Since 1985 the best salespeople have utilized their intelligence, insight, and creativity to design brilliant, customized solutions to their customers' most challenging problems and issues.

What Do Customers Want?

What are customers looking for today? They are looking for more! More information that can help their business. More ideas that will keep them on the leading edge. More knowledge and resources that will provide them with a strong strategic and competitive advantage so they can seize their "unfair share" of the market.

They seek relationships with salespeople who are eager to invest their entrepreneurial spirit and energy in their endeavors. They appreciate salespeople who are trend-conscious visionaries and can anticipate the possibilities of tomorrow in the challenges they face today.

Visionary Selling is more than a new spin on solutions selling. It goes beyond repackaging the concept of value-added selling. Visionary Selling is a new sales paradigm that offers the customer advantage and opportunity through *value creation*. What is value creation? You create value for the customer's business by identifying opportunities that will increase profits, expand market share, or enhance competitiveness. These are benefits that an executive will always want to discuss.

For example, several years ago Pacific Bell received a request for proposal from a large retail department store chain. Since the RFP was for a PBX system, which Pacific Bell does not sell (they lease central office services, called Centrex), they realized they had to change the rules of the game to encompass a greater scope of services and value. Since they were working with the CFO, they focused more on financials than on telecommunications. Their proposal included an entire network for voice and data transactions, presented the benefit of saving store space that would improve a key indicator of store productivity per square foot, and calculated the drain on return on assets of a capital expenditure to buy a PBX. These actions all added value to the proposal by considering key retail business processes.

Then they went one step further: They analyzed the relative productivity of various store departments and determined that china, silver, and crystal sales produced the best margins. What does this have to do with telecommunications? They *created value* by designing a way to significantly increase the store's market share for wedding gifts with an automated bridal registry. Shoppers could view an on-screen display of gifts the couple had registered for and see what had already been purchased, so duplications and returns were reduced.

When you identify market opportunities or profitable ventures that will be of benefit to the customer, you transcend "adding value" and "create value" where it did not exist before. Pacific Bell transcended the specific guidelines of an RFP to create additional value for the customer's business, and was rewarded with a $10 million contract.

Every company is interested in new product ideas or market opportunities that will produce new revenue streams. For example, Eastman Kodak began manufacturing one-time-use cameras. These cameras have produced additional revenue for Kodak since 40 percent of the pictures taken would not have been taken otherwise.

> Follow the "bloodline" of your prospect's business to identify areas where information is exchanged: Who are its suppliers? How does it add value to those supplies for their customers? How does it distribute their product?

Begin with Their Vision

Five years ago a good friend who owns a sign shop was telling me about her experience in selecting a CPA to handle the accounting responsibilities for her business. Over cappuccino she explained that she had chosen three to interview and from those three had selected someone she felt strongly about. I asked how she had made the decision and still remember her words: "I chose the one who had a vision for my business."

This statement was prophetic. Five years ago the only people talking about vision were crazy entrepreneurs, referred to by Tom Peters, author of *In Search of Excellence* and *The Pursuit of WOW!*, as "maniacs with a mission." Since that time, however, a very positive trend has emerged in corporate America. Throughout this period of reengineering, reorganizing, and rightsizing, corporations have invested critical time and energy on three key activities:

- Defining their vision
- Identifying their values
- Focusing on their core competencies

The New Vision-Led Corporation

Corporations are involved in a major transformation, from being "structure-led" to being "vision-led." Until recently they were arranged in a hierarchy, visually defined by the ubiquitous organizational chart. This structure provided clear direction and order. A cataclysmic change has rocked the business world as it relinquishes the "command and control" of the hierarchy and embraces the obscure non-structure of pursuing a vision. We are moving into an era of shared power, where each employee shares an understanding of corporate objectives and accountability for results.

Corporate computer systems provide a good analogy to this process. Just ten years ago computer power and all the company's intelligence were contained and controlled in a carefully monitored, closely guarded room that housed the mainframe. Today, computer networks distribute the company's intelligence through all the personal computers in the network. In the same way, the vision and values of the company are distributed throughout the organization, with each employee possessing a part of the picture and a piece of the puzzle.

This transition may be positive, but it is hardly painless. Polarized forces are warring in corporate America: Control versus freedom, order versus chaos, hierarchy versus empowerment. The battle between these conflicting ideologies has drawn first blood, and troops are assembling on each side of the field of battle. Many are left in the middle, not sure which side to join but certain they want to get out of the middle of the battlefield. They feel anxious, unsettled, and, most particularly, vulnerable. They are desperately seeking something to connect with and someone to follow.

What can they connect with? Who can they follow? To determine the focus of leadership for the 90s, a poll of Fortune 500 CEOs published in the April 1989 issue of the magazine asked what would characterize top leadership abilities in the decade to come. Their number one response was vision. In *Competing for the Future,* Hamel and Prahalad claim the real key to future market leadership is the ability to envision and then create tomorrow's competitive reality.

Corporations have invested enormous amounts of thought and energy into deciding who they are and where they are going. They may not be sure how they will get there—they may not even be positive where they are today—but they have a vision of the future, they know what they stand for, and they know where they excel.

As a prelude to a program I was presenting to Silicon Graphics, I attended the first day of their North American field organization sales meeting. The CEO, Edward R. McCracken, spoke these words: "We might not know how it will happen or how we will get there, but we sure know who we are and where we are going!" Imagine the value a salesperson provides to customers by understanding "who they are and where they are going." This is the power of Visionary Selling: Create an alliance with the vision, values, and core competencies of your customer or prospect.

This is true value-added selling. The value added is your intelligence, creativity, and focused commitment to *their* business. Imagine how your customers will respond when you combine your stellar product knowledge with a thorough understanding of their business issues and then add the additional ingredient of *alliance* to fulfill *their* vision.

An understanding and alliance with their vision and values transcends the superficial "schmoozing" of the typical business relationship, usually an attempt to establish rapport by discovering common interests in sports and hobbies. Creating an alliance with their vision and values produces a bond that is necessary and appreciated in today's chaotic business environment.

Extract the prospect's vision from the annual report of the company and include it in your cover letter. Establish the connection between its vision and your proposal.

Aligning with Vision Achieves a Strong Connection

Salespeople understand the need to foster business relationships that will provide value to the customer and to themselves for many years to come. In the current environment of rapid transition and constant change, we must find something enduring and consistent to base that relationship on. A company's vision, values, and sense of purpose were designed to be the bedrock that supports a shifting and evolving business environment. Regardless of what business situation exists in two years or five years or ten years, the vision will be intact. In 1991, looking ahead one hundred years, Roy Vagelos of Merck & Company said:

> Imagine that all of us were suddenly transported to the year 2091. Much of our strategy and methods would have been changed by developments we cannot anticipate. But no matter what changes might have occurred in the company, I know we would find one thing had remained the same: the spirit of Merck people. I know that because Merck's dedication to fighting disease, relieving suffering, and helping people is a righteous cause—one that inspires people to dream of doing great things.

When you create an alliance with the vision, values, and core competencies of your customers, their business becomes your business. Their dreams become your dreams. Their goals become your opportunities. By understanding who they are and where they are going, you can say, "This is how I can help you get there." You create a business alliance that will provide value and support into the next millennium, no matter what the world looks like by then.

How to Align with Vision

Aligning with vision to achieve a connection is a visionary sell. Let me provide an example. Jon Wampler is the president of PacifiCare of California, the state's leading managed care organization with more than 1 million members. As with many corporate executives, he is a frequent motivational speaker at various meetings and dinners. Jon's message is "Anything is possible!" and he illustrates his belief with stories of amputees scaling fourteen thousand–foot peaks and senior citizens completing races all the way across America. The common denominator among these peak performers is the belief that anything is possible.

After one of his talks, Jon received a telephone call from a man who began by saying, "I heard you say that anything is possible." He went on to explain that he owned a very small company, and his goal was to work with a very large company: PacifiCare. He believed that anything was possible. He captured Jon's attention by connecting with his personal vision and his professional values.

He then said, "This is what I want to do for you." PacifiCare had a printing problem; their oversized documents would not fit into file folders. Before speaking to Jon he had devised a solution. He got the business.

You may be thinking: So what? That is basic solutions selling. But he *first* captured attention and established a business alliance based on a vision connection. This solid bond will earn him the opportunity to transcend to a higher level of value creation for PacifiCare in the future.

Understanding who your clients are connects you with their heart and soul. Resolving a troublesome problem establishes you as a true business partner who has earned the right to become part of their team. Suggesting a transformative idea positions you as a visionary whose ideas merit attention and consideration.

Discover the CEO's favorite slogan or pet phrase (his or her administrative assistant may assist you here). Connect with this slogan or phrase in your voice mail message or the first paragraph of your letter.

Visionary Selling in the Movies

In the movie *Working Girl,* we see a classic example of Visionary Selling. Tess McGill, the working girl played by Melanie Griffith, has a heart of gold and a head for business. She is hired as an assistant to Kathryn Parker, played by Sigourney Weaver. Kathryn pretends to be mentoring Tess; actually, she is stealing her ideas. Tess has been thinking a lot about a company called Trask Industries, which has two major goals: to become an established player in broadcasting by buying a TV station and to resist a hostile takeover attempt by a Japanese competitor.

Tess realizes that by buying a radio station, Trask Industries would achieve both goals. They would get their foot in the door of broadcasting and could begin to establish a base. Since the FCC prohibits foreign ownership of radio stations, any possibility of a takeover would be eliminated.

Imagine Mr. Trask's reaction when he hears this insightful, nearly perfect business idea from a total stranger. Whether he bought the idea or not (he did), he would certainly be impressed that someone invested so much time and creative thought in his business before ever meeting him, working with his company, or earning a single dollar. He would undoubtedly want to stay in touch and hear her ideas in the future. And that is the whole idea!

Visionary Selling in Real Life

Imagine you have been assigned a new sales territory. The good news is that the territory is Rochester, New York, headquarters of Eastman Kodak. The challenge is that Eastman Kodak has an established relationship with your competitor, and no one from your company has been able to establish a foothold.

What would you do? This is the story of Leo Rivera of Silicon Graphics and how she tackled the challenge. Although she had never heard the words Visionary Selling, Leo implemented the selling model in a story bound to become a sales classic.

Leo believed there was a natural alignment between Kodak and Silicon Graphics. She set out to understand Kodak's business and to identify specific areas of commonality. She began by visiting the library and scanning news articles, whereby she identified the highest-profile executive who had been recently hired by the company. Carl Gustin, then director of Digital and Applied Imaging and now chief marketing officer, became her first target.

After reading Carl's goals and objectives when he joined the company, Leo developed a sense of who he was and where his attention was focused. She also obtained Eastman Kodak's annual report. After reading the letter written by George Fisher, CEO, she glimpsed the synergy between George Fisher's vision and Carl Gustin's goals and objectives. She learned the background for many of the ideas Carl had articulated in his interviews. She could see the alignment and understood why Carl Gustin had been chosen for the position over other potential candidates.

Target an executive in your prospect's company as your entry point. Hint: The last executive hired is often representative of current executive-level focus and philosophy.

Leo followed an intuitive hunch in designing a strategy to connect with the executives of Eastman Kodak. Silicon Graphics has an eighteen-wheel tractor trailer called the Magic Bus. The inside is a technological marvel, equipped with Silicon Graphics workstations featuring three-dimensional graphic software. To enter the Magic Bus is to step into a world of high-tech wonder and futuristic fantasy. The Magic Bus was designed to amaze technical types at trade shows and conventions, and it is very effective.

Even staid engineers and introverted scientists say *wow!* However, it had never been used for an executive event. No one had ever imagined it in that role.

Leo completely customized the vehicle. She selected applications of specific interest to Kodak, identified through her research. She borrowed and bought Kodak equipment to integrate into the systems. She approached Kodak employees who were current customers or end users of Silicon Graphics' systems and asked them if they would like to staff the bus for a day. When she told them they would have exposure to their own senior executives, they eagerly signed on. She even remembered to ask them to wear their Kodak badges.

Ed McCracken, the CEO of Silicon Graphics, had been featured on the front cover of a *Business Week* issue titled "The Gee Whiz Company." George Fisher was also featured on the cover of *Business Week* a few months later. On one entire wall, Leo created a montage of color copies of the two covers, showing the faces of these visionary CEOs side by side.

Elegant invitations to tour the "Multimillion Dollar Showcase on Wheels" (the new executive-level name for the Magic Bus) were printed on textured stationery. The following was printed at the top:

> In a recent speech to a group of employees,George Fisher concluded with a quote from Niccolò Machiavelli's *The Prince:*
> *"There is nothing more difficult to take in hand, more perilous to conduct, or more uncertain in its success than to take the lead in the introduction of a new order of things."*
> And, he added, more invigorating.
>
> In the spirit of Mr. Fisher's vision, Silicon Graphics and our Kodak partners bring you a Multimillion Dollar Showcase on Wheels!

The invitations offered "Special Executive Hours by Invitation Only." As each executive responded, he or she was assigned a specific time.

On the big day, the Magic Bus was parked in the parking lot of Eastman Kodak headquarters, in full view of everyone in the building. A sign was produced that said WELCOME KODAK, and it was angled so that anyone looking down from the tower could see it. As the executives arrived and signed in, each was met by a Silicon Graphics executive who acted as a personal escort through the barricades and into the vehicle. Each Silicon Graphics executive had a script to follow that was focused on Kodak's issues, objectives, projects, and goals. An executive summary was presented to each executive at the end of the tour.

Invitations had been issued to the press for specific times, and television camera crews were present throughout the day. The rest of the day following the special executive hours turned into a mob scene as the executives went back and gave their direct reports: "You've got to go down there and see this."

Leo obtained a follow-up appointment with Carl Gustin and had an opportunity to discover his hottest issues and explore his future intentions. She invited him to Silicon Graphics' corporate headquarters in California to meet with executives from her company, and he accepted. He then agreed to take her to meet with George Fisher to present ideas for projects they had developed together.

Before her meeting with George Fisher, Leo called those who reported to him directly; they represented every area of the company, from research and development to manufacturing to finance. She said to each of them, "I will be meeting with George Fisher. Before I do, I would like to meet with you so I understand your issues and will be able to represent your interests." Ninety percent agreed to meet with her.

Her preparation was so thorough that by the time she met with Fisher, her information base was possibly more comprehensive than that of anyone who had ever met with him before. During the meeting she was able to say such things as "Based on my meeting with research and development, I know you are focused on [confidential information]."

Has Leo Rivera's goal of capitalizing on the alignment between Eastman Kodak and Silicon Graphics been realized? Well, these things take time. The following quotes taken from several television news reports are perhaps the strongest testimony to Leo's power and influence:

> What do Jurassic Park and Kodak Park have in common? For Eastman Kodak, it could be a big part of the company's future.
>
> The "Multimillion Dollar Technology Showcase on Wheels" is in town to show folks at Kodak what Silicon Graphics and Kodak can do together.
>
> Kodak and Silicon Graphics, two companies with leaders who see the world the same way . . . digitally.

The Last Resort

I have made an ironic discovery in talking to people about Visionary Selling. Many salespeople have told me stories of times when they had tried everything, pulled out all the stops in their sales efforts, and had gotten absolutely nowhere. As a last resort, out of utter desperation, they changed the focus to the customer's dreams, goals, or visions—and got the business.

AT&T has an approach called "Common Bond Selling." A sales manager, Loreene Ledingham, accompanied an account executive on a customer call to resolve a pricing issue and try to save the account. Loreene began talking about the customer's business and values, and how AT&T's values aligned with the customer's. She didn't talk about price at all. The account executive was perplexed, because Loreene usually talks about business and applications. The customer's posture, which was initially rigid and standoffish, changed completely. The account was saved *without the price issue ever coming up.*

Peter Allocca is a sales rep with Exide Electronics, the world's number one manufacturer of uninterruptible power supplies (UPS). One of the world's largest suppliers of PBX systems sells Exide UPS under their brand name as a value-added, complimentary product line to protect the phone switches they sell to their customers. The PBX company had been working on an RFP from Price Waterhouse, which had a corporate vision to create a nationwide network of virtual offices to reduce expenses and increase profitability and shareholder value. After extensive research, Price Waterhouse selected them for the PBX's but an Exide rival for the UPS's.

As part of a joint sales call, the PBX rep and Peter called on the computer facilities manager and project engineer. Once the facilities manager realized who Peter was, he became irritated. "I've already made my decision. Why are you wasting my time?" he demanded. Instead of presenting the technical and performance reasons to switch or responding with lower pricing, Peter began asking about the project. The computer facilities manager began bragging about his "baby" and explained the company's vision behind the virtual office concept. One aspect of the vision was the firm's intention to stick to its core competencies of accounting and consulting, and minimize involvement with maintaining data centers.

Peter immediately responded with the following: By choosing an Exide solution, Price Waterhouse could consolidate all of its telecommunications and power protection solutions configuration and maintenance under one contract and with only one point of contact. It became clear to the facilities manager that he could support his company's vision and reduce overall maintenance complexity by going with the proposition. A purchase order for $600,000 in revenue potential was generated within fifteen minutes of the beginning of the sales call.

The selling approach of last resort often works miracles. Why not try it first?

Selling Beyond the Solution

Imagine the competitive advantage Visionary Selling offers to you as a salesperson competing for business with other salespeople who are also intelligent and committed. The key to achieving top sales results is differentiation: successfully communicating something you offer that the competition does not. Today, you are selling solutions. What is your competition selling? Solutions. Where is the differentiation?

By discovering and understanding their vision, values, and core competencies, you have broken the code. You have integrated new paradigms into your sales methodology. You have vaulted to a new level of participation and collaboration with your customer. And your customer will notice.

* ANNUAL REPORT
* CEO VISION/CATCH PHRASES
* FORM ALLIANCES W/ OTHER EXECS W/IN FIRM

CHAPTER 3

Think Like a CEO to Sell to a CEO

Visionary Selling is particularly effective when selling to the "C" level of the corporation. And just who is the "C" level? The "C" level is any executive with a C at the beginning of his or her title: CEO, CIO, CFO, COO, CAO.

Top-performing salespeople understand the value of top-down selling. Top-down selling *creates* top-performing salespeople! If you want to become more effective in selling your ideas and solutions, begin by establishing a relationship with someone *above* the decision. Picture the results that are possible when that person becomes your coach and champion. Focus on the increased attention you will receive when you are connected at the top. Imagine the strong impression you will make when your information or your call is forwarded to the decision-making level.

If you doubt this, stop right now and make a call to the CEO of any corporation. Explain the reason for your call to the CEO's administrative assistant. (Any reason will do; just make one up.) Now notice what happens when your call is forwarded. You will probably discover that, by some miracle, your call is answered by a person and not by voice mail. The person who answers will probably bend over backward to assist you. Amazing, isn't it? The explanation: Most executives and managers can identify the origin of a call, whether from outside the company, internal, *or from the boss's office*. And when a call is from the boss's office, the level of interest and attention tends to increase.

When your call or information or proposal is forwarded from a top executive or when you are personally referred by a top executive, the interest and attention of everyone you work with will increase!

To achieve success in sales today, it is essential to establish relationships at every level of the organization. You must communicate value at each relevant level. The "C" level seldom makes the final technical decision, but it often determines the context for the sale. It is up to you as to which way you will travel: the easy way, from the top down, or the hard way, from the bottom all the way up.

I remember the moment I experienced this sales "aha!" I was meeting with the vice president of sales for a large electronics company. I presented my services and received what I perceived as a mediocre response. Suddenly he excused himself from the room and returned with the CEO. He began presenting my recommendation to the CEO with considerable enthusiasm and obvious support for my proposal. When he finished, the CEO said, "Let's do it." Those three words were the only words the CEO said while he was in the room, but they were certainly the words I wanted to hear! And I have seen the world of sales in a new light ever since.

What does the "C" stand for? Chief! And who is the chief? The person who can say, "Let's do it!"

What are the benefits of establishing an alliance with the "C" level?

- You receive more attention and better treatment when connected at the top.
- It at least doubles your chances of getting the business.
- The partnership will be based on bigger, broader issues and will last longer.

The "C" Level Is More Accessible

Reengineering the Corporation, the book by Michael Hammer and James Champy that initiated many of the corporate changes our customers and prospects are dealing with today, states that "not the least of the changes set off by reengineering is the opportunity and necessity for a shift in the role of a company's senior executives. Flatter organizations move senior executives closer to customers and to the people performing the company's value-adding work."

Reengineering and flatter organizations have moved senior executives closer to us as well! The top levels of the organization are more accessible than ever before. The traditional organizational chart that defined corporate authority and relationships in the past, protecting and isolating executives from anything but executive-level issues, is being replaced with a structure that resembles a wheel. A vision or idea or project is the hub of the wheel; each function or individual or team interacts through its connection and contribution to the hub. As a result of a more open and flexible structure, executives are more involved with customers, projects, and teams.

"In traditional companies, organizational charts map the circuitry of permissible conversations and commands. Information technology abolishes the hard-wired routes, substituting flexible networks that enable people to communicate instantly and freely. Linear sequences give way to simultaneous and iterative processes. A good idea can provoke an uninhibited cascade of reactions in a hundred expected and unexpected places."

John Kao, *Jamming: The Art and Discipline of Business Creativity*

You Must Know What the "C" Level Is Thinking

What would it take for the good idea that provokes a cascade of reactions to come from you? This is the ultimate goal of the Visionary Selling process. However, understanding the "C" level's issues and objectives is a prerequisite for good ideas. You must spend enough time with the "C" level to achieve an alliance and

CEO/PRESIDENT

CFO CIO COO

VP VP VP VP

MGR MGR MGR MGR MGR MGR

Organizational Chart of Traditional Company

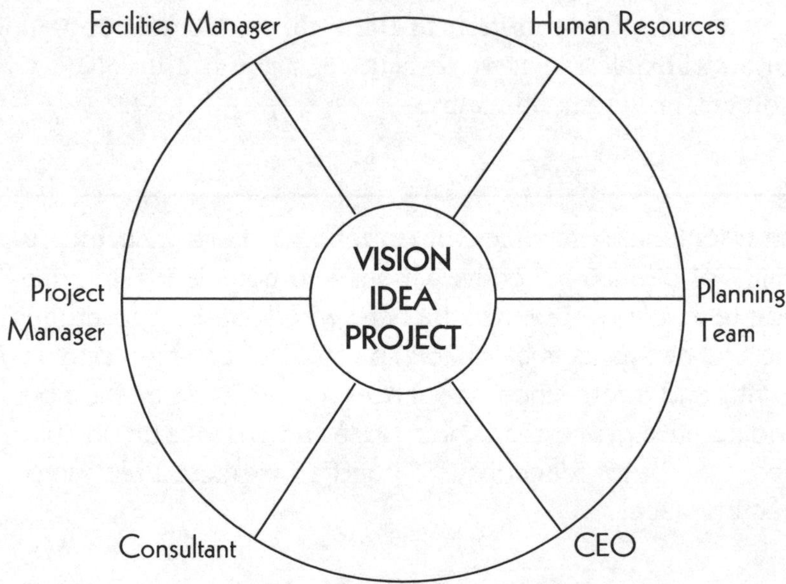

Networked Structure of Visionary Company

to understand the context of their decisions. (Remember Leo Rivera's meetings with George Fisher and his direct reports?)

What do I mean by the "context of the decisions"? I remember learning in college that the media do not make decisions for the public or influence public opinion as much as people believe. They do, however, define the agenda. They determine what it is we are forming opinions about, and they do this by their selection of the topics they focus on. In the same way you cannot force the final decision, but you can define the agenda by bringing your topic to the attention of the CEO in a way that gains his or her interest.

I was recently speaking at a regional sales conference of one of my clients. One of their top executives was addressing the group, and I sat in on her presentation. She mentioned meeting with the CEO to determine their focus for the sales force in the upcoming year. When she finished, I introduced myself and asked, "When you met with the CEO, was helping your people sell more effectively to top executives one of your goals?" In an intrigued and thoughtful manner, she responded that it was not but perhaps it should be.

Some of your prospects may have a confusing organizational structure. Ask someone in an administrative function to diagram it for you and to draw arrows between executives and managers who have close working relationships.

What if you are unable, despite your best efforts, to access the executives of the company? It is still essential to know what the "C" level is thinking and planning. We lose business when we don't know what is going on at the top, because the "C" level are the drivers of the organization. They articulate the vision. They formulate the strategy. They create the agenda.

Every presentation and proposal will benefit from an alliance with the "C" level vision. References to the vision, execution of the strategy, and alliance with the executive agenda resonate with each decision maker you meet. Why? Everyone in the organization knows the song that top management is singing, and everyone is dancing to that tune!

What is that tune? It is a very popular ditty called "Produce Profits."

Ask questions to determine what your prospect's senior executives use as measurements of success (that is, units sold, inventory turns, asset turnover ratios).

The Mandate to Increase Shareholder Value

What is the number one objective of every publicly traded company? To increase shareholder value. The corporation may be focused on expanding global presence, producing new product lines, increasing market share, or reducing cycle times. These are goals. The objective of these goals is to increase shareholder value.

Why is increasing shareholder value so important? Public corporations are owned by a constantly shifting group of shareholders. The value that shareholders place on a stock determines the company's market capitalization, or what the company is worth. And the company's market capitalization influences such critical factors as access to capital, representation in the media, and ability to attract and retain quality employees.

Market capitalization has an impact on a corporation's capacity to thrive or even survive. During the last four quarters, for example, Cisco has achieved a 22 percent net profit margin on sales of $4 billion. As a result, Wall Street and investors love the company, and the stock price is high. This gives Cisco a market capitalization of $40 billion. To stay ahead of the competition, Cisco has freely used its $40 billion market capitalization to buy promising companies, spending $5.5 billion in stock during the past eighteen months alone. Market capitalization is like money in the bank. Market capitalization equals market power!

The value of a public company is reconfigured every single day when the stock exchange closes. It is the fundamental law of supply and demand. If more investors buy the stock than sell, the price goes up. If more investors sell the stock than buy, the price goes down.

Before an appointment or call, check the stock price of your prospect's company. Congratulate your prospect when it is up. Ask why when it is down. This will lead to many revealing conversations.

The "C" level regularly multiplies the number of outstanding stock shares by the day's closing price to determine what the company is worth. For example, Bill Gates owns 141 million shares of Microsoft stock. Based on today's closing price of $90, Bill's personal stock is worth $12,695,000,000. Wow! The stock price was up ⅝. Bill made $88 million today. On another day the stock could plunge $3—for example, if reports of quarterly earnings were below analysts' expectations. On that day Bill's stock would lose $423 million in value. What do you think Bill's mood would be when he is losing $423 million, even if the loss is only on paper? Do you think top executives at Microsoft would move quickly to avoid the possibility of disappointing analysts (and Bill) again?

A primary factor that drives stock price is expected earnings. Why do earnings have such an impact on stock price? Because the average investor does not have the time or knowledge to understand management's long-term goals and objectives. Investors cannot keep up with the business activities of the companies whose stock they own, so they rely on outward manifestations to determine what is going on within those companies, namely, quarterly earnings and other financial measures of performance.

The average investor has very little influence on the decisions and strategies of the executive level. Institutional investors are another story. Financial managers who oversee large pension funds, bank trust departments, and the assets of insurance companies have become very aggressive in demanding improved stock performance. This intense scrutiny focuses the attention of corporate executives on maximizing their company's stock prices.

Business leaders complain that Wall Street and investor preoccupation with short-term performance indicators, such as quarterly earnings, undermines their ability to focus on long-term strategies. The following is an example of the result, summarized in an excerpt from *The Wall Street Journal:* "A lower-than-expected profit rise at Motorola, Inc. spooked investors. That news sent Motorola shares tumbling $7 in heavy trading. The decline clipped some $950 million from the company's total market value. Even as the company's executives profess to manage for the long term, investors can't help but react to the short-term reality."

Motorola is not the only company that has watched in horror as its stock price plunged when it missed an earnings projection. In *Crossing the Chasm,* Geoffrey Moore states, "It is not uncommon for a high-tech company to announce even a modest shortfall in its quarterly projections and incur a 20 to 30 percent devaluation in stock price on the following day of trading." Even a slight hiccup can demolish the value of the stock and thereby reduce the paper value of the company.

Just as a change in one number of a spreadsheet reverberates through the remaining numbers, a change in stock value reverberates through the company. What effect does a decrease in market capitalization, or the value Wall Street places on the company, have on the company's finances? Available capital may be withheld. Credit lines may be reduced. Interest rates on existing debt may be increased. And when investment dollars are reduced, top executives begin to wonder if they will have the money they need to invest in the business today in order to succeed in the future.

How does this actually affect day-to-day operations? Job postings may be replaced with hiring freezes. Layoffs may be considered. Research and development budgets may be cut. Financing for key projects may be eliminated. Advertising and marketing may be reduced. Employee morale may dip as stock options and retirement funds lose value. Like a shock wave, ripple after ripple impacts the company's financial strength, market performance, and employee outlook.

"C" Level Performance Appraisal

Who does the CEO answer to? The board of directors. Who does the board of directors answer to? Shareholders, particularly large institutional investors. Corporate boards are under considerable pressure to increase stock value, which they communicate in various ways to corporate executives.

If the company's value is increasing, based on Wall Street value, the "C" level will experience job security. If the company's value is decreasing, there had better be a good reason—or those on the "C" level could be out the door. The CEO position used to be like that of a king—practically for life. Not anymore! Poor shareholder returns increasingly trigger top leadership upheavals at major corporations. Think of the times you have read recently that a company simultaneously announced lower-than-expected quarterly earnings and the resignation of the CEO to "pursue personal interests."

According to John Kao, author of *Jamming,* "Every morning of their ever-shortening tenures, CEOs and their entourages awaken to the clarion call from the financial pages: 'So what are you going to do for me today?'"

The Council of Institutional Investors, whose combined assets exceed $1 trillion, compiles an annual list of underachieving companies—corporations in Standard & Poor's 500-stock list with the worst total shareholder returns over the past five years. Half of the council's latest tally of twenty poor performers have named a new chief executive officer or interim CEO in the past three years. The council's pension funds often use the target list as a bargaining lever in pressing for changes in management, strategy, or corporate governance, and it seems to work. The year after being listed, these previously underperforming businesses experience an average total return of 21.1 percent, which is 11.6 percentage points higher than the S&P 500.

In a *Fortune* magazine article entitled "The Wealth Builders," Betsy Morris states, "There are all sorts of ways to grade a chief executive. Look at his return on equity. Calculate his return on investment. Take quarterly note of his earnings growth. Rank him against his peers. Rank him against his industry. Or judge him by the most fundamental measure of all—how much wealth he has created for his shareholders."

Profiled in her article is the late Roberto Goizueta, the CEO of Coca-Cola who concentrated on shareholder wealth as the company's ultimate goal. A video monitor at the entrance of the main building at corporate headquarters shows the stock price, updated several times a day. It is the first thing employees see each morning and the last thing they see when they go home at night. Goizueta revamped Coke's pay incentive plan to make millionaires out of even lower-level managers who succeeded at creating wealth for shareholders. I would say his focus was quite clear. And what about Goizueta personally? More than 99 percent of his personal wealth was tied up in Coca-Cola stock.

The board of directors of many public companies has implemented compensation plans that link "C" level salary to increases in stock price. Bonuses are often directly proportional to increasing profits and stock price. The powers-that-be have sent a clear message of where they want top management to concentrate their attention and energy. In a survey published in the September 1995 issue of *Inc.* magazine, a close link was discovered between compensation and company performance, which *Inc.* claims mirrors a strong national trend. According to *Inc.*, "Sixty-six percent of the CEOs said that a bonus made up some part of their compensation last year, and one third said that a bonus constituted at least 25 percent of their pay. That finding is not surprising, since with this group growing the company is often the prime motivation, which means growing the value of the company."

Michael Eisner earned $203,010,590 in 1993, the highest income of any executive ever. This phenomenal windfall was the result of salary plus bonus plus exercising stock options, which he was awarded for increasing Disney's value 1500 percent during his first nine years on the job!

Obviously, this high-risk/high-reward compensation package puts tremendous pressure on top executives. You can dry your eyes and put your tissue down, however. The *average* stock option from a major company in 1995 was valued at $1.52 million. The *average* bonus paid by a major company in 1995 for performance in 1994 was $1.22 million, a 39 percent increase over the previous year. Why? Because quarterly earnings, shareholder return, and stock prices were all strong.

Now you understand why profitability is a key driver for the "C" level. How can you use this information to sell to them? First, let's examine what does not work.

Some salespeople obtain an appointment with an executive and, without conducting thorough research or specific investigation, attempt to persuade the executive that their product or service can increase revenues or reduce costs. Top executives are much too savvy to fall for this. The entire executive team has invested their collective intelligence and expertise in determining how to accomplish these objectives. After all, this is their job! They take it seriously. If you walk in with a canned presentation and a canned solution, you will be laughed out the door (politely, of course).

When you obtain an appointment with an executive, ask about his vision, strategy, and plan to increase revenues and reduce costs. Trust me, he does have one. Thousands of hours of his time and the time of experts in several disciplines went into its design. He understands the issues far better than you ever could. Then follow his lead in helping him execute the strategies he has already designed.

For each prospective client, begin a list of the company lexicon used in conversations with you. Refer to it before each call or appointment. By talking like the client, you will understand the client better.

Don Tremblay of Xerox was assigned to a Fortune 500 company with tremendous potential. Its revenue had been flat, however, and it was involved in a downsizing process. Xerox had been receiving cancellations on existing orders from many divisions. Don met with key executives and listened as they described their strategy to utilize business process reengineering to refocus on core competencies and improve the efficiency of critical components of their business.

Imagine a typical salesperson involved in this conversation. One of your largest potential accounts is downsizing and cutting costs. You have already lost business, and this is definitely going to mean fewer orders for you in the immediate future.

Although it initially meant less business for him, Don supported the company's downsizing and cost-cutting efforts. He designed creative ways to support the existing level of service while reducing costs. He even migrated the company from older to newer technology, increasing the level of service at no additional cost.

The payoff? Several years later Xerox has captured 100 percent of the business in several business segments. They have one hundred of their employees working on-site at the company. The company has been upgraded to digital technology, and by using "print on demand" processes they have improved the timeliness and flexibility of their materials while reducing costs. Next year should be the largest growth year Xerox has ever had with this customer.

Xerox aligned with the company's vision to become lean and mean, and supported vital strategic elements for future success, although it meant a short-term revenue reduction for them. By connecting with the vision and working through the process with them, Xerox is positioned to share the growth that is the result.

Intrinsic Factors of Success

Many companies have achieved legendary success by focusing on intrinsic factors, such as a sense of purpose. In *Built to Last: Successful Habits of Visionary Companies,* James C. Collins and Jerry I. Porras analyze the habits of eighteen exceptional companies that have "stood the test of time." They list as Myth #3: "The most successful companies exist first and foremost to maximize profits."

The authors state that "contrary to business school doctrine, maximizing shareholder wealth or profit maximization has not been the dominant driving force or primary objective through the history of visionary companies. Yes, they seek profits, but they're equally guided by a core ideology—core values and sense of purpose beyond just making money."

The Formula for Communicating with the "C" Level

You know the profit and loss (P&L) formula: Subtract expenses from revenues. If you have something left, it is a profit (the more, the better). If the number at the bottom of the column is a negative, you show a loss. Anytime you can increase the top line (revenues) or decrease expenses, you will improve the bottom line (profit). But if you are not a numbers person or can't imagine talking this stuff with a CEO or CFO, here is a secret:

> The "C" level increases profitability by leveraging the resources of vision, values, and core competencies.

What if you are working with a visionary company that is focused on purpose and values, and does not consider profits the primary indicator of success? Simply reverse the formula to change the emphasis:

> The "C" level leverages the resources of vision, values, and core competencies to increase profitability.

Now you have the formula. You know what makes them tick. Does your product or service have a positive impact on their people, productivity, or products? Will it increase their power, position, or profits? Does it connect with their vision, values, or core competencies?

Each individual at the "C" level has learned to take these factors into account when making decisions that have significant impact on the corporation. For example, the CIO function was once considered so complex and technical that it was insulated from the typical business concerns. In 1994, Deloitte & Touche surveyed more than four hundred CIOs of U.S. and Canadian organizations in all industries. Three-fourths of the CIOs named communications and networking technology as an important enabler, because "empowering people with newer, more flexible information technologies goes hand in hand with successful redesign of business processes." In other words, technology decisions are now linked to executive issues and objectives. The chief information officer in today's corporation is expected to identify strategies to increase sales, decrease expenses, create a competitive advantage, improve customer satisfaction, and increase market share.

Sam Palmisano, CEO of IBM's Integrated Systems Solutions Corporation, confirmed this change in focus by saying, "To be a great CIO today, you need to be a businessperson and help the company apply technology to business goals. The top priorities are access to technology, skills, reengineering, revenue growth, and shareholder value."

The "C" Level Worldview

Assisting our customers and prospects with key business issues and strategic opportunities requires a solid understanding and education in areas of business management and business finance—where some salespeople fear to tread. As a result, many large corporations are educating their salespeople in top-level business management courses, "mini MBAs."

Patrick Kelly, CEO of Physician Sales and Service, claims, "We don't hire salespeople or truck drivers or computer specialists. We hire CEOs—people who want to develop a broad-based knowledge of the business and who are prepared to act on that knowledge. But CEOs are made, not born. This year we'll invest $3 million to educate our people in business fundamentals."

If your company is not offering this benefit, it is up to you to develop these vital skills. Before you can understand and interpret the "C" level's vision, you need insight about the world that those at the "C" level live in. You must learn to think like they think. You must see issues through their "worldview." And you do this by reading what they read, listening to what they listen to, and going where they go.

A reading list is included at the end of the book. *The Wall Street Journal* is a prerequisite for Visionary Selling, since it is read by nearly every executive in the United States. The front page alone is worth the subscription price. By simply glancing at "What's News" every day, you will be better informed than many of your competitors.

Various columns and articles that appear throughout the week are a gold mine to assist you in identifying hot business issues, patterns, and trends. Pay particular attention to the editorial page. Many of the letters are written by top executives in public corporations. You will gain insight into how they think, trends and developments that intrigue them, and issues that are bugging them. You will become aware of their issues and viewpoints, and more comfortable with the objective of communicating with them directly. By immersing yourself in these thoughts and issues, you will begin to think like a CEO!

> Stories sell! Choose business stories that illustrate your point. Reduce the stories to sound bites or analogies, and rehearse until you can present them succinctly for maximum impact.

I know some of you couldn't face a business day without your cup of coffee and *The Wall Street Journal.* Others may be intimidated by this publication or feel they don't have the time or money to become a regular reader. Try this: Stop by a local library every day for the next month and spend ten minutes perusing this paper. If you don't feel the time invested was of value, discontinue the activity. If you do, subscribe.

I once read that an individual who spent one year going to art museums daily would rival the world's leading art critics by the end of the year simply by *exposure* to art. Business is the same way. By the end of one month of investing ten minutes daily, you will exceed the average businessperson in your grasp of key business issues and developments.

Select one of the others, at least once a month, and peruse it while on a plane. Carry periodicals in your briefcase; if you are kept waiting, you can use the time wisely. While you are sitting in a corporate lobby, pass on *People* magazine to read the industry magazines and trade journals they have available.

Go to the library reference section and ask for the *Standard Periodical Directory.* Look up specific industries you are focusing on by classification, or choose specific periodicals in the alphabetized section. Compile a list of the ones that interest you; call each one and ask for a sample copy. Now you can review your stack of potential sources of information and choose several that appeal to you for subscriptions.

Keep your eyes and ears open for opportunities to listen to executives speak or to mingle with them at business events. Conferences and conventions often feature executives as keynote speakers sharing their vision for the future of business and the industry. Business programs on television and radio feature interviews with top executives. CEO forums and round tables, such as those held by the Association of Corporate Growth, provide opportunities for executives to share ideas and information.

By surrounding yourself with information about how the "C" level thinks and feels, you will begin to understand its unique perspective on business and on life. You've heard the cliché, "It's lonely at the top." That is probably a myth, but it is different at the top. Top executives bear a tremendous amount of responsibility and accountability. Top executives are generally extremely committed, competitive, and perfectionistic. They have bold visions and high standards. They long to associate with others who share their worldview and understand their needs. Are you willing to prepare yourself to accept the charter of "C" level counsel?

The "C" Level Frame of Reference

In my work with clients I see salespeople gaining an understanding of top-level issues and objectives. Most salespeople have learned that the fastest way to alienate an executive is to present a data dump on the features and benefits of the salesperson's product. They understand that to communicate with an executive, you must focus on adding value by resolving an issue or achieving an objective. What is different about communicating at the very top levels, and how can Visionary Selling assist you?

The difference is the "C" level's frame of reference. The frame of reference at the executive level is between five and fifty years, depending on the needed planning horizons of the business. The focus is not on what is going on in the business today or even this year or next. The mandate is to scan the business horizon searching for information and ideas regarding business opportunities and business threats that are not yet visible to the average person (or, it is hoped, to their competitors).

Recently, I had the opportunity to talk with Robert Peebler, the president and CEO of Landmark Graphics. Bob is leading the charge to computerize the oil and gas industry with his company's product of sophisticated software systems. Does Landmark have a mission? You bet: "To lead in creating a new era of finding and managing oil and gas reservoirs through integrated information solutions that provide a dramatic business advantage for our customers."

When I asked what he thought separated top executives from others in the company and from salespeople, Bob talked about planning horizons. He claims that the levels of management in a company depend on levels of complexity that the executives must deal with, which are best measured by time horizons. A division president will most likely be dealing with plans that are five to ten years ahead, while the CEO of the same corporation may be envisioning and planning how the business will look twenty and perhaps as far as fifty years ahead.

To understand how this changes the focus, think of your company. At the lowest level, the planning horizon may be zero to three months. A receptionist, for example, is dealing primarily with issues such as high calling volume today and the need for new equipment in a few months. At the top level, your CEO has a much longer planning horizon. He or she is playing an integrating role and focusing on the future of your industry, marketplace trends, research and product development, and how to integrate all the corporate functions strategically to assure long-term success.

Herbert D. Kelleher, CEO of Southwest Airlines, has established a reputation as a wild and crazy guy known for outrageous shenanigans and over-the-top actions. He appears to be a real "in the moment" guy, and yet he expresses a long-term frame of reference in this statement: "Our focus is far beyond. What are we going to be in the year 2015?"

This small change in focus changes everything! If you have ever met with a top executive and watched her eyes glaze over as you discussed short-term savings or increases in productivity, you now understand why. The executive is simply not focused on the present reality. Have you ever watched a futuristic movie and emerged from the theater feeling disoriented in a modern shopping center? This is how that executive felt while listening to you.

Think of the "C" level mind-set as a split screen. On one screen is a vision of the future, five to twenty years from now. On the other screen is a short-term picture of quarterly results. Everything else is in between and is not in the executive's frame of reference.

Features and benefits of a product or service are in between. For the most part, problems and solutions are in between. No wonder we have been failing to capture the attention of the "C" level.

What Do CEOs Fear?

The "C" level is preoccupied with the business of leading the company and the responsibilities of leading its people. These activities can rob them of the vital time necessary for observation and contemplation, the companions of creative thought.

Those on the "C" level are aware of the ultimate executive danger: Spend so much time leading people that you lose sight of where you are headed. Become so immersed in the inexhaustible responsibilities of corporate leadership that you forsake the ultimate responsibility of managing a profitable, competitive venture. The "C" level lives in fear of spending corporate time and energy on building a better mousetrap, only to discover that a competitor has discovered *how to keep mice from coming into the house in the first place!*

This is why Lewis Platt, CEO of Hewlett-Packard, restructured his time to include meetings with a few customer groups each day to discover what his company is doing right and what can be improved.

Microsoft Versus Netscape

Conjure up a picture of Microsoft, one of the largest and most powerful corporations in the world, led by the richest man in America. How do you think Bill Gates and other Microsoft executives felt when *The Wall Street Journal* referred to Netscape as an "upstart rival to Microsoft"? How do you think Bill reacts when he reads news articles wondering how Microsoft missed the emergence of the Internet and identifying Netscape as the company that defines the Age of the Web?

I'll bet it makes him fighting mad. Why? Because a new communication medium, social phenomenon, and business opportunity like the Internet should never have gotten past Bill or

Microsoft. This business had their name on it. If only someone had whispered in their ear, given them a clue, and convinced them to sit down and listen several years ago.

In case you've missed the Netscape story, here it is: Netscape began in early 1994. In the spring of 1995 it went public in one of the most impressive initial public offerings of all time. Although the company had just $16 million in revenue and had never earned a profit, by the end of the day it was valued at $2 billion. One of the cofounders, James Clark, went to sleep half a billion dollars richer than he had woken up. Another, Marc Andreessen, accumulated $60 million in stock on that one fabulous day of the twenty-fourth year of his life. During the next few weeks, stock in this start-up soared from the IPO price in the low twenties to over $100!

So what's my point? I do not tell you this story to make you jealous—although I am! The point is, in business today you cannot afford the luxury of taking a breath. A short period of relaxation can be deadly. Business is moving very fast and has major revisions in the players every month. IBM and Dell Computer were sinking and are now rising to the top. A huge company like Microsoft is engaged in a market share war with a small start-up called Netscape, which few people had heard of before 1995.

The "C" Level Is Listening

As a result of these tales and others like them, the "C" level is listening. Social and business trends begin with the man on the street, and the executives know it. The hottest business ideas today may be in the head of a young skateboarder in Venice, California, or a high school dropout on the streets of Chicago, Illinois. Or yours! Opportunities are not only where you would expect to find them but everywhere. Considerable risk exists in ignoring creative people who want to discuss ideas with you.

A *Business Week* cover story on Scott McNealy, CEO of Sun Microsystems, claims McNealy frets that with so much on his plate, he'll be blinded to the next big thing: "We're so frantic with everything going on right now that we know we're missing something."

The Quest for Business Innovation

In *Reengineering the Corporation,* Michael Hammer and James Champy discuss the need of companies today to move fast or they won't be moving at all. To do this they have to be "looking in many directions at once. Executives *think* their companies are equipped with effective change-sensing radars, but most of them aren't. Mostly what they detect are the changes they expect."

Conversely, in *The Renewal Factor,* Robert H. Waterman, Jr., talks about the opposite type of company, which he calls renewing companies. "They get their passport to reality stamped regularly. Their leaders listen. They are open, curious, and inquisitive. They get ideas from customers, suppliers, front-line employees, competitors, politicians—almost anyone outside the hierarchy." They call this process informed opportunism, a fusion of the rational and the random that is an energy source which corporations can tap as they seek to renew.

This quest for transformation and renewal has generated a plethora of unorthodox activities. Companies such as Boeing, AT&T, and Wells Fargo Bank have used theater groups to bring emotion into their meetings to spark innovation. German computer giant Siemens Nixdorf Information Systems has assembled teams of young fast-track employees to perform as "sparring partners" to the management board. Called the FutureScape team, their role is to challenge the board and provide ideas and opinions on breakthrough technologies, demographic trends, and competitive forces that will define the computer market in the year 2025.

Through a one-on-one interaction with a member of the board, each contributes a genuine voice in shaping corporate strategy.

Skandia, the Swedish financial services giant, has created a future-focused think tank of "knowledge pioneers." Their goal is to present a vision of the future to Skandia's corporate council of senior executives.

In 1995, 3M received the National Medal of Technology. This award, the highest honor bestowed by the president of the United States for technological achievement, recognized 3M for nine decades of innovation. Delve into the background for 3M's creative spark, and you will discover the name William McKnight. He led 3M from 1914 until 1966, and his maxims are still followed in the company today:

> Encourage experimental doodling.
> Listen to anybody with an original idea, no matter how absurd it might sound at first.

Begin your cover letter with a quote from an admired company, such as the one above. I have an original idea that may be of considerable value to you. Are you willing to listen?

The title of an article in *The Wall Street Journal,* "Little Guy Gives Big Player Idea, Wins a Seat on Company's Board," says it all. David L. Moore, the young owner of a small company, approached a $285 million company with a business idea. "He brought a concept to us that we fell in love with, that we thought was brilliant," said the chairman, who utilized Mr. Moore's idea and then rewarded him with a board seat and a $3 million compensation package.

Of course, you are not looking for a board seat or a multimillion-dollar check (or are you?). You simply want to . . .

- Penetrate higher levels.
- Present visionary ideas.
- Outperform your competition.
- Establish a business alliance that endures.

Presenting bold and brilliant ideas is your ticket to the game.

In *Competing for the Future,* Gary Hamel and C. K. Prahalad state, "The new solutions emerge not because the challengers are more efficient than the incumbents, but because they are substantially more unorthodox. They discover the new solutions because they are willing to look far beyond the old. Any company that cannot imagine the future will not be around to enjoy it."

Many consultants earn $250 an hour or more to help companies imagine the future. Companies such as Inferential Focus, nicknamed the CIA for CEOs, furnish business intelligence on anomalies and trends for an average annual fee of $24,000. But at these rates their services really add up. In this era of corporate cost-cutting, executives are looking for substitutes that add the same value at a lower cost.

Design a one-page newsletter filled with information on business trends, including a few off-the-wall tidbits. Fax it to the executives of your prospect's company on the morning of their executive meeting.

In ancient Greece this function was performed by an oracle in the shrine at Delphi. An oracle is defined as a person or agency considered a source of wise counsel or prophetic opinions. Although the oracles of Delphi were not advice-givers in the strict sense, they did help the Greeks discover answers to their issues. The oracles stimulated them to look inward and consult their own intuition and wisdom. The problem was defined in a new context, allowing the Greeks to see it in a different way. Previously unimagined possibilities would emerge.

What if you could offer the same value as a high-level consultant without the big fee? What if you could demonstrate that you understand what the company is and where it is going? What if you could also demonstrate that you possess the intelligence, insight, and creativity to offer imaginative ideas and valuable approaches? Would the potential of receiving a transformative idea from you be enough to get you in the door?

Visionary Selling casts you in the role of oracle, delivering information and predictions to their doorstep as an added value of your service to them.

How common is this approach in selling today? It is very rare. Herb Carter, executive vice president of sales at Siemens Stromberg-Carlson, a division of Siemens Corporation, listened as a top executive from one of their largest customers said, "Your people have never come to me with a business solution." Now you and I realize this cannot be true, but perception is everything. Why don't they think salespeople have come to them with a business solution? Their idea of a business solution and a salesperson's idea of a business solution are two different things!

When I spoke to CEOs while researching this book, I heard the same thing over and over. This comment from Bob Peebler of Landmark Graphics is typical of the answers I received when I asked when and how a salesperson had aligned with their vision and offered an insightful or valuable idea:

> Unfortunately, I can only give bad examples rather than good examples. I have not yet had one salesperson approach me with a "higher level" idea. They always come with features/functions or a "canned" solution that is looking for a home. I would enjoy just once having a salesperson start the discussion with a better understanding of what we are trying to accomplish and probe me for a deeper understanding of our challenges. We have plenty of them,

but I sometimes feel as if I am in a desert where original ideas are water. I am still waiting for the innovative visionary sales approach, versus a mirage called a solution that is designed to benefit the selling company versus mine. I suspect that most CEOs are just as thirsty. Can you imagine having a lemonade stand in the desert? That is what Visionary Selling is all about.

The "C" level is listening. Talk to them!

* LEARN BUSINESS STORIES TO WHERE U CAN EFFECTIVELY USE THEM IN SELLING
* UNDERSTAND CEO'S VISION VALUES & CORE COMP
* CUSTOMIZE LETTERS W QUOTES FROM A RESPECTED COMPANY
* CEO'S ARE FEARFUL OF MISSING THE "NEXT BIG THING"

PART II

TOOLS AND TEAMS

CHAPTER 4

Five Unique Strategies to Penetrate the "C" Level

What is the first goal of Visionary Selling? To help the salesperson get inside so that he or she can advance the dual causes of the prospect company and the salesperson's own company. What is required to get inside? For an answer, let's look at the question from an executive's point of view.

What Do Top Executives Want from Salespeople?

What would a top corporate executive gain from meeting with you, a salesperson? What would motivate that executive to spend valuable time with you?

Could it be your brilliant flair at presenting the features and benefits of your product or service? Not likely. The "C" level is not easily impressed by bells and whistles and is many levels above the level where buying decisions are debated.

Perhaps it's your ability to solve their most critical business problems? Absolutely not. Top executives are not responsible for solving problems. They have others working for them whose future employment depends on keeping problems off their desk.

The "C" level is focused on and committed to a dual mandate: Formulate a vision for the future that strategically positions the company and lead the company to continually increasing levels of profitability. No easy task. What is required for the executives to achieve these objectives?

First, they must create an organization that attracts and retains top-quality personnel. Next, they must produce or distribute a product or service that sells. They must define advertising campaigns and marketing strategies that are relevant and effective. They must satisfy their current customers better than the competition can, and convince prospective customers that they will outperform the vendor who was selected in the past.

And now you are asking for some of their time. Why would they even consider your request? There is only one reason that the "C" level would be interested in meeting with you. Remember WIIFM? What's in it for me? They will meet with you if they believe you have something to offer that will be of benefit to them. The sooner you tell them what it is, the sooner they will pay attention.

> Design an introductory statement that will gain the respect of an executive while it also communicates your style and value, such as, "I know it would be a waste of time to come to you with a sales presentation or a canned solution. I understand that you know your business far better than I ever could. But I do have a good mind and a fresh perspective, and I promise to listen carefully to all information you share and to transform that information into insightful ideas."

A recent survey conducted by a large communications equipment manufacturer involved talking to top-level state and local government officials to identify what those officials considered important. Please note that officials volunteered this information because they felt that it was essential for sales representatives to know what issues to discuss in initial sales meetings. Study this information carefully. I believe the answers are indicative of the focus of all top executives.

QUESTION:

Upon initial contact, what factors might persuade you to meet with a salesperson?

ANSWERS:

My need for information and knowledge.
The reputation of the supplier and past experience with them.
A knowledgeable sales representative who knows my business operations and understands our business needs as well as my personal needs as a top-level official.
The professionalism of the salesperson (a consultative selling approach).
The title or position of the person asking for the appointment.

QUESTION:

When contacted by a sales representative regarding a major purchase, what do you want to talk about?

ANSWERS:

My organization's goals, needs, and key plans.
Industry trends, key issues in the market, what similar organizations in my industry are doing.

From the answers to this survey, it seems top executives are looking for a high-level, focused information exchange. They want to discuss their organization specifically to let you know what they need and how you can assist them. They want to discuss industry, market, and competitive trends so that they can benefit from information and ideas you have which may be of value to them. Isn't this really quite simple?

Michael D. Newman, corporate account manager at 3M, designed their corporate account management process. The mission statement is "to develop, facilitate, and manage long-term mutually beneficial business relationships between 3M and selected strategic corporate accounts." Mike has attended seminars for salespeople on gaining executive access and claims none of the executives he has met with have asked him any of the questions that were covered in the seminar. They want to know about 3M, and they want to know how 3M can help grow their business. Period.

Mike has a response to this query that generates productive communication about needs and opportunities. When a top executive asks what he can do for them, Mike says: "Candidly, nobody has all the best knowledge, engineers, or R and D in the world. There are gaps in technologies in both of our companies. Through a cooperative effort we can help fill those gaps."

This comment leads to specific discussion. Mike pulls out a piece of paper to outline immediately the framework, some of the steps required, and the beginning of an action plan. The collaboration has begun.

What Do Salespeople Have to Offer?

So what do you bring to the party? What can you offer top executives who have a continuous supply of almost everything they need? Can you help them with your enormous power in the business community? access to capital? influence with the media? important contacts? Probably not.

Here is what you can offer: fresh ideas, a novel outlook, the ability to challenge their assumptions, shift their paradigms, and help them see issues in new ways or tackle strategies with new insight. They are always on the lookout for unusual ideas. They will entertain "wet behind the ears" types for the fresh perspective they offer. According to John Kao in *Jamming,* a recent survey showed many executives rank inventiveness at the top of their list of corporate priorities.

George Bennett, senior vice president of sales and marketing at ATC Communications, claims that top executives assign the ultimate value to knowledge. They are always interested in learning—about their competitors, about new technology and its applications, and even about what is going on at other levels in their own company.

It's a big job, but someone has to do it—someone with courage! If you stick to the safe route, you are absolutely redundant with the yes-men who already surround them. A top executive cannot expect wild or breakthrough ideas from those who report directly to them. With their career and livelihood at stake, direct reports simply have too much to lose to challenge the boss. Moreover, they are a product of the same corporate environment, immersed in the same corporate culture, and working with the same corporate information.

According to Al Ries and Jack Trout, authors of *Positioning: The Battle for Your Mind,* "Like kings, chief executives rarely get honest opinions from their ministers. There's too much intrigue going on at the court." Think of your relationship with your current boss as well as relationships with previous bosses. How often did you rattle their cage? If you are like me, you probably waited until you had a specific agenda with no other alternative available for its achievement. Very few employees look for opportunities to challenge their bosses just to keep the creative juices flowing.

Flowing creative juices, however, are exactly what corporations require to stay afloat in today's business environment. And they know it. In *Competing for the Future,* Hamel and Prahalad maintain "it is not enough for a company to get smaller and better and faster; a company must also be capable of getting different." The top executive who is focused on getting better and faster needs your help to see ways in which the company could also get different.

Go Out on a Limb

This is the most important tip you will receive on communicating with the "C" level. (It is also the most frightening.) If you get this, you will thrive with Visionary Selling. If you don't, you will flounder. To offer value to the "C" level, you must . . .

- Go out on a limb.
- Challenge their assumptions.
- Smash their paradigms.
- Communicate controversial ideas.
- Become a "CEO catalyst."

You must identify an element or an aspect of your solution that is controversial, provocative, or counterintuitive. This aspect will guarantee that your proposal stands out from the others. It will position you as a salesperson who is more intelligent, more insightful, more visionary, and certainly braver than all the others. Whether or not the idea connects, you will be perceived in a new light.

I know, I know: This is scary stuff. Not only are you going to meet with an important high-level executive where you are bound to feel at least a tiny bit intimidated, but I am insisting you present at least one idea that is *provocative.*

What do I mean by provocative? The word *provocative* comes from the latin *provocare,* to challenge. The dictionary definition is "to cause deep feeling, to stir to action." Isn't this exactly what you are striving for when you meet with an executive of a prospect's company?

It worked for defense lawyer Jennifer Keller. In 1992 she was elected secretary of the Orange County (California) Bar Association despite the fact that thirteen former bar presidents had endorsed her opponent. How did she achieve this upset? Her campaign literature included the following: *"kicked out of Girl Scouts, expelled from Catholic school for placing kick-me tag on bishop's rear."* Three years later Jennifer was named bar president for 1996.

A touch of controversy hits the mark with the "C" level. Scott McNealy, CEO of Sun Microsystems, acknowledged this when he said, "I want Sun to be controversial. If everybody believes in your strategy, you have zero chance of profit." Scott and others like him have risen to the top by seeing things before others do and having the courage to act on those visions. They intend to stay at the top.

It requires a lot of effort to stay ahead of everyone else, and a lot of energy to continuously replenish the supply of fresh and exciting ideas. A visionary is always seeking resources that will assist in the quest. Being a visionary is hard work!

In *Built to Last,* James C. Collins and Jerry I. Porras state that "comfort is not the objective of a visionary company. Indeed, visionary companies install powerful mechanisms to create discomfort—to obliterate complacency—and thereby stimulate change and improvement before the external world demands it." That is why the leader of Oticon Holding A/S, Lars Kolind, proposes a radical leadership concept: To keep a company alive, one of the jobs of top management is to keep it *dis*organized. When his company needed breakthroughs, he understood a fundamental reality: Breakthroughs "require the combination of technology with audiology, psychology, and imagination . . . the ability to think the unthinkable and make it happen."

Crossing the Chasm author Geoffrey Moore endorses counterintuitive thinking and actions for companies striving to progress from struggling start-ups to mainstream market winners. He tells the story of Sun Microsystems, which adopted a strategy of open systems at a time when every competitor attributed its success to the opposite strategy—maintaining an advantage through proprietary systems. IBM, which had utilized open systems in order to get a PC to market quickly, had experienced severe market erosion as a result of this action when customers began buying IBM-compatible systems, or clones, at significantly lower prices than IBM could offer. Sun selected a counterintuitive strategy that had negatively impacted a competitor and turned it into a clear market advantage for them.

Collect stories of business successes that came about through adverse circumstances, unusual ideas, or strange approaches.

The Provocative Story Penetrates

It is the provocative story that penetrates. Think of a time when someone startled you with a wild idea or a bizarre suggestion. You may have responded defensively, even with hostility, at the time, but I'll bet you kept thinking about it, mulling it over in your mind. You might even have sought the person out to find out more.

The tried and true bores the "C" level, but the power of the unexpected garners attention. Why are these executives fascinated by Tom Peters? He has become one of the most influential business writers and speakers in the world by challenging every assumption they hold dear, thereby providing new windows for them to view a changing world.

I interviewed the CEO of Fluor Corporation, Leslie G. McCraw, while writing *Secrets of Peak Performers.* He told me that in 1986, when he assumed leadership of the company, they had just undergone a difficult merger. The industry was depressed, and Fluor was losing a lot of money.

Les's vision was to build an organization that would be able to confront and respond to challenges never before faced. Ann McGee-Cooper, a consultant from Dallas, Texas, who works with corporate leadership teams on culture change, approached Les and suggested creativity training that included unorthodox approaches such as inviting elementary school children to brainstorm with his management team on key issues and problems. Les invested in this training, which became the foundation of high-level innovation within the company and contributed to a stunning financial turnaround.

Ann McGee-Cooper presented a provocative idea to the CEO of an $8 billion corporation during an extremely tense period. A compelling and counterintuitive approach won her the opportunity to connect and to serve.

Counterintuitive, provocative, controversial: These qualities are attention-getting in an era when it is almost impossible to capture attention. Use them to your advantage as you seek to penetrate the "C" level.

The Essential Ingredient: Attitude

In the world of Visionary Selling, the most essential ingredient is your attitude. Visionary Selling requires exceptional self-confidence, chutzpah and moxie. If you already have it, simply follow the process. If you don't, developing an attitude of intense self-confidence is the first step.

Why is attitude so important? To answer that question, we must examine the people at the "C" level and find out who they are.

But first, let's confront our fears. Why are we nervous when we contemplate calling a CEO on the phone or scheduling an appointment with a CFO? What are the underlying assumptions or anxieties that get in our way?

If you look closely at your emotional responses, you will realize that you assume top executives are different from you. If you are really honest, you will admit that you think they are better than you. They have reached the top levels of corporate influence and power, so they must be more intelligent, more knowledgeable, and more effective than you are. You might even feel they are on a wavelength completely different from you; they are of another species, perhaps even superhuman.

"C" Level People Are Human!

Shock! "C" level people are human. No more and no less. I would like to share a personal story that illustrates their "humanness." When I was writing *Secrets of Peak Performers,* I requested permission to interview John Crean, founder, CEO, and chairman of the board of Fleetwood Enterprises, the number one manufacturer of recreational vehicles in the United States. He lives in a forty-thousand-square-foot mansion, the Village Crean, set on four acres of some of the most valuable real estate in the nation, the Back Bay of Newport Beach. When I asked John where he would like to meet, he replied, "The house." Oh, to be in a position to call a forty-thousand-square-foot mansion "the house"!

On the big day I drove up to the twenty-foot-high scrolled iron gates and spoke my name into the intercom. The gates swung open slowly. I entered the compound like Alice in Wonderland, driving along the cobblestone road in awe, parked my car, and approached the massive front doors of a beautiful colonial mansion. I knocked. Nothing. I knocked again. Again, nothing. I was just beginning to panic when the door swung open, and there was

John Crean. He was dressed in his pajamas, flustered and apologetic. He had overslept. Would I come in and wait for twenty minutes while he showered and dressed?

Imagine, the CEO of a humongous company standing before me in his pajamas. From that moment on, I saw CEOs in a new light.

Have you ever been told to imagine people who intimidate you in their underwear? I guess the theory is that this imagery somehow levels the playing field. The underwear part seems somewhat demeaning, but imagining them in their pajamas gives a warm, fuzzy connotation to a potentially stressful situation.

Why did I share this story? It is essential for you to muster feelings of confidence before you begin calling on top executives. In my work with clients, this issue is the first to surface. How do you overcome natural feelings of insecurity and apprehension if you have never communicated successfully with a top executive? How do you catapult over the fear barrier to achieve productive encounters, which will provide confidence and motivation to continue the process?

Why not think back to your first sales calls. Do you remember how frightened you were to pick up the phone for your first cold call? Do you remember, as I do, hoping the phone line would be busy or no one would answer? And now you are a master of the sales process. You don't dwell on the possibility of rejection. You are confident of the value you offer.

To interact successfully with executives, you must move through the same learning curve. You will feel apprehension initially. You might make a few mistakes at the beginning. You will improve, grow, expand in ways you never imagined possible. You will become a more successful salesperson, selling at a far higher level of the corporate value chain.

Obtaining an Appointment with the "C" Level

How could a competitive and highly resourceful top executive say no to an investment of ten minutes of time if there is a possibility that you will provide a significant idea or valuable information? How can you gain their attention to score that first vital appointment? Let's explore five strategies to gain the interest of a top executive (or anyone at a decision-making level).

#1: Meet Them out of "Context"

Remember the fictitious example of Visionary Selling from the movie *Working Girl* in Chapter 2? If you saw the movie, you may recall the way Tess communicated her idea to Mr. Trask. She crashed his daughter's wedding and maneuvered her way into a dance with him. This is Hollywood stuff, of course, and I don't recommend it for you, but this illustration includes a key element that we can adapt to our goal. Tess approached Mr. Trask "out of context." He wasn't expecting a business idea, so he didn't have his guard up. He was open, relaxed, and receptive. By the time he realized what was happening, he was hooked on her idea.

If you specialize in a specific industry or target market, attend the industry trade shows. Top executives are often accessible with time to talk.

When I decided to conduct a CEO study for my first book, the little whiny voice in my head, as well as many friends and associates, asked this question: How will you get appointments with these very important and busy people? As I pondered that question, I attended a meeting. The Orange County Red Cross was honoring the CEO of a large company that was a major corporate sponsor of theirs. During the CEO's introduction, an impressive story was told about him. I congratulated the CEO after his speech and followed up with a letter a few days later. I began the letter with a reference to the story and mentioned this as the reason I had chosen him to interview. It worked; I got the appointment! I then used his name to get the second appointment, and on and on until I had met with all twelve of my intended subjects.

Exposure to the "C" level outside of typical business settings is invaluable. A story in *The Wall Street Journal* profiled Diane Dawson of Dawson Sales Company, who learned early on that selling succeeds on relationships. She became involved with volunteer work for the Chicago Symphony and other organizations, working her way up to the trustee boards so she could hobnob with local CEOs. She became the first woman elected to the board of an elegant dining hideaway, and she took up golf so she could participate in the more open business discussions she had observed on the links.

Involvement with charitable and community organizations is one of the best ways to meet and mingle with executives.

Where do your targeted "C" level executives congregate? What community or industry organizations are they involved in? What would it take for you to meet them first on this turf and then ask permission to contact them with your idea?

Does your company sponsor events for top executives where information or a program of special value to the "C" level are offered to entice their participation? Would your company be interested in sponsoring or participating in a golf or theater benefit to support local charities or organizations?

Design a strategy to plug into a network of CEOs. Once the CEO job was practically for life, and CEOs tended to go "heads down" into their work. They interacted with their board, a handpicked team of managers, and a tight group of advisors. With today's average tenure of 2.3 years, there is a growing awareness among CEOs that they are vulnerable. As a result, top executives are building a network of relationships. Every single external relationship they can develop may be of critical importance when they are in "career transition"—including a relationship with you. You are working in their industry, you are out and about, and you have relationships in other companies that might be of value to them in the future.

Identify organizations that attract top executives and people who work with them, such as the Association for Corporate Growth. The people who work with them can provide an access point to a CEO. Venture capital firms, executive recruitment and outplacement firms, law firms, accounting firms, and insurance carriers have solid relationships with CEOs. They sell CEOs all the time. How can you provide value to them in exchange for a networking relationship that could lead to an introduction? You could, for example, assist an executive recruiter by letting him know when an executive position opens up in your customer's company or in your own.

#2: Telephone/Voice Mail/E-mail

If your idea is a hot one, nothing matches the immediacy of the phone for two reasons:

1. You can get right to the point.
2. If the other person doesn't bite, you can get right off the phone.

It is likely, of course, that your call will be directed to voice mail. Voice mail systems have many foes who love to complain and to criticize the impersonal nature of the technology. I am not one of them. I attribute several of my greatest sales successes to an ability to use voice mail as the powerful tool it is. It becomes a powerful tool when you learn to communicate a message that is bold, energetic, intriguing, and concise.

I imagine you have at least one prospect you have been unable to connect with despite months of trying. Either the prospect is totally uninterested, or you are stuck at a level below the decision. What do you have to lose? When you leave a voice mail message for the final decision maker or someone above that level, one of two things will happen. The prospect you have called will ignore the message, and no one will ever know you called. Or the person will respond to your message or instruct someone else to, and you will be in the game.

Use the following format to design a voice mail script for that prospect. (Think of how impressed you will be if that "hopeless case" becomes a customer after you use this process!) After writing the script, rehearse a few times before placing the call. *Do not read from the script;* you will sound stilted and boring. You must inject your thirty- to sixty-second message with all the confidence and charisma you possess. I suggest standing when you leave the message; the increase in power and energy in your voice will be noticeable and can make the difference.

Format to Design Script

I am calling to [specific information pertinent to his or her company].

Would it be of benefit [an insightful idea or intriguing suggestion]?

My name is ______________ from ___________________, and I will follow up with a phone call to your administrative assistant on __________ to arrange a conference call or appointment.

Sample Script (software company salesperson to health services CEO)

I am calling to address an issue you mentioned when you spoke at the December meeting of the Association of Management Consultants. You said that you felt out of touch with Generation X and weren't sure how your company should be marketing health care services to them.

If you were talking to a person of Generation X today, what advice would you give? I believe you would counsel them on the importance of relying on themselves instead of a corporation to take care of their needs and to view themselves as the CEO of their own small business—called Me, Inc.

I have an idea for a new type of health care service based on a personal, independent policy and marketed over the Internet. My name is Ralph Resource with ______________, and I will follow up with a phone call to your administrative assistant on ______________ to arrange a conference call or appointment. (This message is forty-five seconds in length.)

What kind of response can you expect from this type of message? Once in a great while you will receive a call back from the CEO's administrative assistant to schedule a call or appointment. More frequently you will receive a call from someone several levels below the CEO, mentioning that your call was forwarded to her and agreeing to talk to you. I believe this is a great consolation prize, but you be the judge.

E-mail is another approach that combines low risk with high reward potential. It is easy to obtain the E-mail addresses of many top executives. Some read their E-mail while traveling or during other periods of downtime. Imagine the connection that could be made if you provided a tantalizing idea for them to mull over during a restless transatlantic flight or a frustrating airport delay. A captive "C" level audience with time to ponder. Hmmmm!

> Search online directories for the E-mail addresses of top executives.

The biggest advantage of both phone and E-mail is that very little commitment or investment of time is required. The prospect doesn't have to decide whether or not to meet with you. The prospect doesn't have to exchange the pleasantries and formalities found in a face-to-face encounter, which often drive business executives crazy as an obligatory waste of precious time.

A phone call to a top executive to present an idea requires only three to five minutes of her time. Listening to a voice mail message from you takes one to two minutes, and reading an E-mail takes even less. If your idea bombs, you can still score points with your concise communication and your courage in presenting an idea to the prospect. As a result, she may be willing to invest the time to meet with you in the future.

#3: Packages

When all else fails, you can send a telegram, package, or other creative attention-getting device. This story is a favorite of mine. Paula Graber, who attended one of my seminars, told of majoring in advertising in college. The dream that got her through four years of stress and sacrifice was this: *The minute I graduate, I will go to work for a top advertising agency.*

As graduation loomed, one of her professors invited executives of the top four agencies to speak to the class. Each of the four was adamant: "We never, ever hire recent graduates. We insist they gain experience, prove themselves, and get their knees bloodied a few times before we will even consider them."

She left campus devastated. She moped all day. Then she got clever. She bought a Barbie doll and removed its arms and legs. She sent a letter to the creative director of each of the four agencies, beginning with this sentence: *"I would give an arm or a leg to work for you."* She included her résumé and either an arm or a leg from the dismembered Barbie.

The result? Four interviews and four job offers! Why? She communicated a "pertinent and provocative story." A creative director is always looking for new, creative ideas and people who can communicate ideas in a novel manner.

A young man named Don was working in the customer service department of a bank, but he had always dreamed of working in the record industry. When he confided his desire to friends and family, he heard the usual sensible advice: "You just can't get into that industry. No one will even talk to you."

He especially loved music from the 60s and 70s, and was fascinated by the compilations of old songs done by Rhino Records. He spent hours at the library doing research and reading articles, and discovered the two founders of the company were colorful off-the-wall characters. He tried a few of the traditional job search practices, but they failed.

He put together a recorded compilation similar to Rhino Records' product and sent it to the president, Richard Foos. Using his voice as a voice-over, he pretended to interview himself. In response to interview questions, a selected phrase from an old song would answer.

SONG: Open the door, Richard.
VOICE-OVER, interviewing Don: Why do you want to interview Richard?
SONG: Get a job . . .

A graphic artist created a box with a door, and the cassette tape was placed on one side. On the other side was a listing of "10 Reasons You Should Talk to Don." A response card with the following was included:

Dear Don:
__ The tape is fabulous. Show up for work on Monday.
__ The tape is great. Let's talk.
__ Don't call me, I'll call you.
__ Get a life, Don!

It took a while, but Mr. Foos's secretary finally called. "Mr. Foos did listen to the tape," she said, but he sent it to the director of human resources who was "absolutely responsible for all hiring." When he called the director, she stated that Richard Foos had suggested she meet with him. She mentioned that his box was displayed on a shelf in Mr. Foos's office.

The interview did not lead to a job, but out of the blue they called him one year later. This time he did get the job. They never forgot him; how could they? Don puts it this way: "I'm famous in this company."

Here is the most important point of this story. Don was uncomfortable with 75% of the process, but he did it anyway. How strong is your desire?

#4: Survey Appointments

Design a survey of three unique and insightful questions, and ask for ten minutes of an executive's time to explore her viewpoint on these issues. I have found that most people, especially opinion leader types, are naturally drawn to answering questions on a survey when the time involvement is minimal and the obligation is clearly defined.

The executive is certain to ask you what the survey is for. You can respond that your company is seeking to discover what top executives are interested in when they meet with salespeople.

You might also tell him that the information will be included in an article you are submitting to a trade magazine or to the local business press—if you are interested in writing an article.

#5 AUDIOCASSETTE

Where I live in southern California, people spend as much time commuting as they do in their office. This may be true with your prospects as well. A great way to capitalize on their uninterrupted, focused time is by recording a teaser version of your idea on an audiocassette. You can demonstrate specific knowledge of their vision, values, and/or core competencies, and explain how that knowledge led to your idea.

Give them the short version of the idea. Ask for ten minutes of their time to communicate and explore it in more detail. This audio recording should be less than five minutes in length. On the outside of the cassette, handwrite "Personalized for Mr. [or Ms.] ______________ . . . 5 Minutes."

Jump Two Levels

If meeting with a CEO seems preposterous to you, jump two levels. Select the boss of the boss of the person you usually work with. Believe me, when you get in there, you will discover issues and perspectives that are different from what you have been dealing with. No wonder you were losing business.

Stop for a moment and think about the following: Who do you sell to now? Who is that person's boss? What does he or she care about? Who is your largest prospect? What is the CEO's vision for that company? What is the CFO's key issue?

Chances are the concerns you mentioned were communicated to you through your contact and not from the source. We all know how information can be distorted when passed from person to person. Remember the telephone game you played in elementary school where a message was passed along? Do you recall how the final message was changed from the original in many pertinent details and sometimes in overall intent after just a few repetitions? If you were to call your contact's boss and engage her in conversation, it is likely that a very different story would emerge from the one you've been hearing.

Let me provide an example from my experience. I specialize in providing an interactive sales training game, Klue, at national sales meetings. I am usually directed to the meeting planner for the event. When I ask the meeting planner about the objectives for a program like mine, I am often told that they are looking for an exciting team-building event that will leave their salespeople feeling enthusiastic. This is understandable, since the meeting planner's success is primarily determined by the analysis of the evaluation sheets, and enthusiastic salespeople provide higher ratings on the sheets.

The person who actually hires me, however, is the vice president of sales, who has a very different perspective. She wants sales results to increase—period. For the most part, whether or not their people have fun or feel enthusiastic is secondary to providing tools that will increase performance. If I am unable to talk directly to the VP of sales to determine *what she feels is required* to achieve a good return on the company's investment, my shot at a successful outcome is greatly reduced. I must satisfy the requirements of both buyers, which I cannot do if I lack information on the perspective and objectives of one.

This is why I resist involvement with the people on the "team" or committee until I have connected with the VP. Once I've had my three-minute conversation with the VP, I have the vital information I need to continue the process. I have learned that it is preferable to wait a year if necessary, go in high, and establish a visionary partnership that will result in a successful outcome, rather than go in low and spend a year or two meeting with people who have a limited perspective or have no authority. This is especially true since while I am bogged down servicing the "team," some smarter salesperson who knows this principle will get the VP on the phone and shove me out forever!

Visionary Selling for a Small Business

You may sell primarily to small businesses. Perhaps you are in a sales territory where you sell to every business, regardless of size, and many of your prospects are small businesses. You may be wondering how Visionary Selling relates to you.

This reminds me of the introduction to a full-page advertisement for Apple Macintosh.

> There is no such thing as a small business.
> Just as there is no such thing as a small dream.

Anyone who has started a business and survived the first few years understands the power of a vision. Small-business owners are obsessed with the vision. Often, it is the only thing that keeps them going. They are incredibly eager to share it with you; it defines who they are. They are incredibly hopeful that you have secrets or ideas or tools that can move them toward it. This is all they think about.

Most businesses are run by middle market CEOs or small-business owner/operators. They are not high flying, and they are not featured in *The Wall Street Journal,* but the majority of them buy every single day. And they will buy from you if you package information and resources targeted to their needs.

When communicating with the owner or owner/operator of a small business, you must speak the language of a small-business en-

> If you work primarily with small businesses, design a newsletter of tips for entrepreneurs. Assemble a team to submit tips, such as an attorney, tax specialist, advertising expert, printer, and so forth.

trepreneur. Who are they? What are they focused on? What do they obsess about? What wakes them up in a cold sweat at 3:00 A.M.?

They are, as a general rule, visionaries. They had an idea or a dream or a product that they felt passionate about, and they are striving to create a profitable business from it. They are driven by the vision, motivated by the bottom line, and tormented by the details of the process. This reality creates their major conflict: They are fascinated by the big picture but succeed or fail based on their attention to detail.

They are personally involved with every aspect of the business. Chances are they are crisis managers—either by choice, because it suits their daredevil personality, or by necessity, because small businesses are fraught with crises.

What kind of crises do small-business owners deal with? Six of the most constant are the following:

- Cash flow
- Sales revenues
- Profit margins
- Managing inventory
- Personnel management
- Meeting payroll

This is not a book on the issues of small-business owners, but one example will illustrate the type of quandaries they deal with constantly, and it encompasses all the issues listed above.

As a result of an aggressive business plan for the upcoming year, the business owner hires a hotshot salesperson to increase sales revenues. The salesperson immediately sells a large account. This account, however, negotiates a 7 percent discount (profit margin), and to encourage the salesperson's efforts, the owner agrees (personnel motivation). As a result of the increased business, the owner must hire three additional employees (personnel management, meeting payroll) and order materials (cash flow).

One of the biggest headaches for small businesses is the lag time between getting the business and getting the payment. In between, they must order materials, pay personnel, and produce the product. For small businesses, profit and cash flow are the lifeblood of the company. We can help these overwhelmed business owners by helping them get focused and by providing innovative and effective solutions to their crises.

Here is an example to get you thinking. Small-business owners are working so hard and running so fast that they seldom have time to focus on a vitally important task: hiring. They procrastinate until they are absolutely desperate and then hire the first living, breathing person who walks in the door. And the person they are most reluctant to hire is a salesperson, since they are often intimidated by the sales process and don't understand the criteria for selecting a salesperson.

What if you helped them in this process? Would that add value to them and position you as a true business ally? Here is an idea that I shared with one of my customers, who has expressed his eternal gratitude: Since successful sales results almost always require strong telephone skills, set up a separate voice mailbox or answering machine. Run an ad listing the job specifics and the telephone number. Record a voice mail message saying, "Since successful sales performance requires strong telephone sales skills, this is your first sales opportunity. Tell me why your sales abilities would benefit my business."

Small-business owners love this idea, because it resolves several issues:

- They do not have to interrupt their daily activities to screen applicant calls; they can do it in the evening at their convenience.
- They can listen to all applicants at one time and weigh their respective sales abilities.
- They can reduce their workload by personally interviewing only the top three.
- They can ask others to review the tape and provide additional perspectives and opinions.

By understanding the challenges and issues that confront small-business owners, we can provide ideas and tools that will help them run their businesses more successfully. In return, they will be receptive to the benefits our product or service provides.

CHAPTER 5

Turning Gatekeepers into Allies

We hear a lot of talk in sales about bypassing the gatekeeper or getting around the gatekeeper. Would you believe me if I told you that the gatekeeper can become your greatest champion and your most powerful ally?

As you work with the top executive levels, it is essential that you support the system 100 percent. To do this you must understand corporate team dynamics. Corporate team dynamics dictate that in order for the company to run in an organized and effective manner, it must utilize a structure that assigns areas of responsibility and accountability to people who are competent to perform those tasks.

Consider a football team. You do not see winning football teams with players running willy-nilly across the field. Each player, whether quarterback or running back or tight end, has a responsibility to his teammates and the team. The defensive linebacker is the gatekeeper.

The gatekeeper position is essential to ensure that corporate employees are able to complete their work rather than spend all their time entertaining vendors who are attempting to complete their own. An effective gatekeeper will also ensure that employees are connected to the people they need to see. It is up to the gatekeeper to decide which is which, and he takes this responsibility very seriously.

When working with the "C" level, you will encounter two specific categories of gatekeepers: the technical buyer and the administrative assistant. Each has a different responsibility, perspective, and even personality style. Let's look at them.

Gatekeeper #1: The Technical Buyer

The technical buyer was introduced and described in the book *Strategic Selling* by Robert Miller and Stephen Heiman. This is the person who can't say yes but can only say no (and usually does). Saying no represents power. The technical buyer loves facts, figures, statistics, benchmarking, and analysis, and is frequently enamored with technology for technology's sake. This is the person most likely to manage RFPs and purchase orders.

If you make contact with the technical buyer first, you risk getting pigeonholed at this level. You are then unable to move above that level without antagonizing the technical buyer. All of us have had this experience, and it is bad news. Why? Because the technical buyer generally cannot or will not make a decision. He or she is often change-adverse and fears the consequences of a bad decision, and so makes no decision at all.

Unfortunately, a technical buyer seldom changes jobs, so once you are affiliated with one, you are stuck. You cannot go over that person's head without causing offense or antagonism. And if you do cause offense, the technical buyer will lie in wait to sabotage you at the exact moment when your defenses are down or you most need support.

Salespeople love results. When you make a call, you want to sell. When you are targeting a company, you want an appointment. Corporate dynamics dictate that everyone in the company will hand you off to the technical buyer who handles your area of expertise. They know exactly the person you should be talking to and are eager to transfer your call. Often, the person they insist you should be talking to is at her desk and available to talk. You could be having a sales conversation, discussing the features and benefits of your product, within seconds!

Resist this. No matter how much you want to talk to someone, no matter how much you want an appointment, no matter how aggressively your manager is bugging you to "get in there," hold out for the decision-making level. It is far more effective to wait a year to reach the top level and achieve a solid alliance based on executive-level issues than go in today and spend that year playing footsie with the technical buyer.

Technical buyers are bad decision makers, but they are fabulous implementers. Most salespeople would love to have these detail people as a partner, to dot the i's and cross the t's. After you connect at the "C" level and gain an understanding of the business issues and objectives, you will often be delegated to the technical buyer level to handle the details. This is what you strive for! This establishes a relationship with a completely different dynamic.

Work with the technical buyer as you would if you had never talked to a top executive in his or her company. Resist the urge to name-drop or refer to your conversations with the bigwigs. You do not want to antagonize the technical buyer by making him feel unimportant or arouse his resistance by reminding him that this was not his idea in the first place. And remember, the "C" level is watching. An important qualification as you develop your partnership with the company is how you work with their "team."

An important tip: Do not forget the technical buyer after the sale is made. Technical buyers take their jobs very seriously and will continue to evaluate alternatives after the project is completed. That is their job, and they do it well.

Remember how hard you worked when your customers were prospects? Right now your customer is someone else's prospect. Your competition is working just as hard today as you did yesterday to get their foot in the door.

What happens to your credibility when you drop your contact

like a hot potato after you have made the sale and completed the project? They are hurt. They feel neglected. The attentive phone calls, the spontaneous gifts, the scrumptious lunches in luxurious settings came to an abrupt halt. They assume that you were just another slick salesperson who schmoozed them until you got what you wanted and then quickly forgot who they were.

Establish a system to provide your technical buyers with the contact, information, and appreciation they crave. It will protect your existing accounts, and the "C" level will love you for supporting the team.

Technical buyers love data. Assemble a one-page collection of relevant facts and figures and fax it to your list of technical buyers (prospects and customers) monthly.

What if you are stuck at the technical buyer level on an existing prospect? Here are four approaches that may help you catapult to a higher level.

1. Supply them with ideas: It is rare to find a technical buyer who would be described as an "idea person." With the current emphasis on business creativity and innovation, a technical buyer feels some apprehension, so when you meet with one, toss out an occasional idea or approach in a low-key, nonthreatening manner. Use terms like "just food for thought" or "noodle this idea." Allow the technical buyer to take your ideas and communicate them to upper management as his own. If he receives a positive response, I guarantee he will want to go one step further and gain recognition by introducing you to the top level.

2. Help them see you in a new light: With your current customers and prospects, strive to demonstrate that you are fo-

cused on broader business issues and can communicate at a higher level than the average salesperson. Remember: They won't take you if they don't trust you. Your contact will not champion your cause and provide entree to the executive level unless she is confident that you have valuable ideas to share which will justify their efforts on your behalf.

Demonstrate that you are capable of communicating at a higher level in the organization. Give the technical buyer tidbits of Visionary Selling by sharing your ideas and insights for her company. Allow her to see you in a new light. This may take time, but consider the rewards.

I remember the first time a telecommunications manager suddenly interrupted our conversation and took me into the CIO's office. I didn't know what I had done and wasn't even sure at the time that this was a good thing. I had communicated several thought-provoking ideas to the telecommunications manager, and he wanted to show me off to his boss. This is what you are striving to accomplish, but a technical buyer won't take you if he can't trust you to communicate on a clear, concise "C" level.

3. Design a "C" level proposal: Develop an exemplary idea or solution. Package it within a high-level, strategically focused proposal that screams for "C" level attention. Depending on your contact's position and relationship with the top level, he or she may persuade the decision makers and executives that you are someone they must meet. Or your contact may present the proposal to them on your behalf. Remember, even when we are unable to connect with the top level personally, we can increase our success ratio by helping the technical buyer sell to them.

4. Establish peer-to-peer selling: Utilize an executive in your company to obtain entry to a higher level in the prospect's organization. This is known as peer-to-peer selling, and it will not antagonize your technical buyer. Position the appointment

as a meeting of the minds of two executive-level individuals who are focused on issues that are more long-term and strategic than the issues the two of you face.

The idea is that these two executives speak the same language, and the two of you will have the opportunity to gain an inside glimpse by sitting in on the meeting. This brilliant strategy not only gets you in at a higher level in the organization but it solidifies your relationship with the technical buyer by positioning the two of you as kindred spirits.

The goal is expressed perfectly in this excerpt from 3M's Corporate Strategic Accounts Program brochure:

> The transactional intersection of two companies—between the supplier's sales force and the buyer's purchasing department—can be a bottleneck. Paperwork, bureaucratic rules, miscommunication, or lack of understanding can reduce a relationship to a series of sales transactions. Loyalty and growth potential decline on both sides.
>
> Or . . . when two companies meet, the point of intersection can be pivotal to each company's growth.

Gatekeeper #2: The Administrative Assistant

The other gatekeeper is the administrative assistant. Here we have a completely different story. The executive administrative assistant can become your greatest champion, even your coach. The very first step is to understand and respect this position and the abilities of the person holding it.

Executive administrative assistants empower the most powerful executives in the world to do the work they do. The leaders of corporate America could not begin to achieve the results they must without assistants who are so intelligent, so intuitive, and so diplomatic that they can create a sense of structure and focus out of chaos.

The first time I entered the executive suite of a CEO's office, I was overwhelmed by a sense of tranquility and calm. No jangling telephones. No blinking computers. No harried employees crowding the hallways and doorways. Just a cool, calm, almost meditative serenity.

How in the world can this be? The CEO I was meeting with is at the helm of an $8 billion corporation with twelve thousand employees and offices in almost every country in the world. And yet there he was in his office waiting for our interview, sitting on a couch in front of a soothing fire in the fireplace—calm, focused, attentive.

Corporations cannot survive and thrive without a coolheaded leader at the helm. This is the environment where a "C" level executive can formulate a vision for the future and design a strategic plan to achieve it. And the administrative assistant—the first line of defense and the last point of refuge to create and protect this environment—is essential to corporate survival and vitality.

Enough said. This very important person with critical job responsibilities appears to stand between you and your objective. There is absolutely no way to get around or go over this person, who is much too smart to allow it. Only one option exists: to gain the administrative assistant's support for your cause. How can you achieve this goal?

Mining for Gold

Take a tip from the profession of gold mining, in which the prospector uses a mesh instrument to sift gold from the surrounding dirt and rock. Is the objective to discard dirt and rock? No! The objective is to obtain gold. Administrative assistants appear to be intent on discarding dirt and rock—you. Actually, they are intent on obtaining gold—you. But you have to demonstrate to them that you are a nugget of gold and not a clump of dirt.

Let me provide an example. One year ago I selected a company

I wanted very much to work with. This company had captured attention and garnered admiration from every aspect of the business community: finance, technology, and consumers. I obtained the name of the executive I wished to speak with. His administrative assistant, whom I will call Leslie, gave the same report every time I called: "He's in a meeting. May I take a message?" Sound familiar?

Since I always communicated my respect for her job and never responded with frustration, after numerous calls Leslie and I began to establish a rapport. I told her more about why I wanted to talk to her boss. I enticed her with potential benefits. I communicated my knowledge of who they were and where they were going, and suggested ways I might be of assistance. We started to become friendly, but even more important, we began to interact like peers. We were united in the same goal: to make her boss look like a hero.

After several months and many calls, the day came when Leslie told me that if I would call back the next Tuesday at 9:30 A.M., she would put my call through. At the appointed time I called to hear her report that he was in a meeting. I did not get upset. I did not remind her of her promise. Administrative assistants have perfect memories; this is how they do the job they do. And then Leslie said, "Would you like me to put you through to his voice mail?"

I knew this was a privilege, because in the months that I had been calling, she had never made this offer. As the phone rang in his voice mailbox, I jumped to my feet to summon confidence and energy. The strategic collaboration I had designed was right in front of me (as it had been throughout the months of calling). I left a clear, compelling, and powerful message in less than three minutes. By the end of the day I had established a relationship with the company. By the end of the month I was doing business with them.

There are ways to bypass the administrative assistant, of course. But first, invest the time and effort to respect and adhere to the channels that were established to protect the executive from unnecessary detail and clutter: the dirt and rock. Demonstrate to the administrative assistant that you are knowledgeable, specific, and offer value, and he or she will acknowledge you for what you are: a nugget of gold. Administrative assistants appreciate individuals who respect the power and value of their position, just as you and I do. They will bend over backward to assist you if you play by the rules. And the executive, who values his administrative assistant over and above all other resources, will appreciate your willingness to work within the system that was established to get the job done.

> Resist the urge to become "chatty" with administrative assistants. This is not the way to establish rapport. Keep all communication crisp and to the point (just as you would with their boss).

Treat Administrative Assistants and Their Bosses the Same

Treat administrative assistants with the same awe, honor, and respect that you extend to their bosses. They are two components of a high-functioning team. Once you are privy to inside information, you will discover that the gap in intelligence and awareness between the "C" level and their assistants is very slim. Generally, it comes down to a difference in their tolerance for the spotlight or to educational and business credentials. A strategic approach is to treat them as two sides of the same coin.

Salespeople commit a strategic faux pas when they regard the assistant of a top executive as a support person with little influence or power. One of my client companies asked me to call the CIO of one of their top accounts to gather information for my presentation. The salesperson sent me a two-page biography on the CIO in preparation for my call. I probably know more about him than his own mother does.

However, when I asked the salesperson to spell the last name of the CIO's assistant, he didn't know. He had been working with this account, an $11 million–a-year customer, for three years. I believe the CIO's assistant is very aware of this discrepancy. When the salesperson desperately needs her assistance, he may have trouble obtaining support.

> **When speaking to administrative assistants, ask for their last names and verify the spelling. This communicates your respect for their position.**

Developing a Coach

Successful salespeople understand the importance of developing a coach or a champion to assist with the challenges of the sales process. The best coach is someone who is involved in the decision or close to the decision-making process. This person can supply you with information or insight not readily available to your competitors and can provide additional perspective on the issues or objectives being addressed. You may need an in-depth analysis of the individuals involved in the decision and their personal needs and motives. You may need advice on timing your call or appointment so that it will coincide with a receptive environment or a responsive mind.

No one makes a more effective coach than an administrative assistant to the "C" level or a top-level executive. He knows exactly what is going on. He knows what information is essential and what is simply "white noise." He knows whom you should call, and when. He knows who your competition is and how you must compete.

Why would an administrative assistant be interested in accepting this role? It may be that the assistant perceives you as a highly qualified, highly professional, highly ethical individual who understands the company and is committed to its success. Or the assistant may feel that you value the critical responsibilities she carries and the vital importance of her work.

When All Else Fails

What if you have worked for months and months to no avail? What if you are working at a lower level, where the secretary or receptionist believes it is his or her God-given right and responsibility to block every call and ensure that no information ever gets through? Here are some tips and techniques that can be used after you have tried everything else and failed.

Call very early in the morning, 6:30 to 7:30 A.M. Call at lunchtime. Call after 5:30 P.M. Call on Saturday. These are the hours before secretaries and receptionists arrive and after they leave, when executives come into the office to work on planning and other issues requiring uninterrupted calm.

A nasty little trend in corporations today is to refuse to give you the name of the person you need to reach. If you call and ask for the CIO, the receptionist will inform you that he or she is not allowed to give out names or does not have titles at the switchboard. When this happens, simply ask for a salesperson. Salespeople are generally willing to provide the information you need.

The Gatekeeper as Ally

Stop fighting the gatekeepers. If you look upon these people as adversaries, they most surely will rise to the challenge and meet your expectations. If you appreciate the job they do, support them in their responsibilities, and shower them with respect, you may discover you don't need to go over or around them. You can walk hand in hand.

CHAPTER 6

Build Credibility and Trust . . . and Keep Them!

Would you agree that most people are looking for a quick fix? Books with titles like *Five Easy Steps to Success* and *Close More Sales, Quickly and Easily* fly off the shelves. We are always on the look-out for immediate results. Instant gratification takes too long. That is why words like *quick, easy,* and *instant* are considered sales and marketing magic.

I could tell you that Visionary Selling is a quick and easy process to increase sales, and you would eagerly sign on. But you know it couldn't be true. All significant achievement requires time and attention. "Work smarter, not harder" implies that working smart is easy. Working smarter might be the hardest thing you've ever done.

Selling to top executives requires significant intelligence, knowledge, maturity, and steadfastness. It is not a passing trend or a fleeting effort. Some accounts could take years to come to fruition; some never will. Since you will be responsible for making your quota in the interim, much of this activity will take place after regular business hours.

The path may be arduous, but the rewards are fabulous. You will develop a network of top executives who respect your ideas and input. More of your sales will be large, profitable, long-term, and of greater strategic value to your company. You will be involved in work that is challenging and meaningful.

Credibility and trust are needed to obtain the critical inside information required for Visionary Selling. Credibility and trust are needed to develop a strategic partnership that will lead to value creation. What will it take to get from here to there? Let's begin by analyzing what doesn't work.

The Danger of Improvisation

The best and worst salespeople share a common skill: improvisation. Salespeople love to confront a challenge and overcome adversity. They enjoy being backed into a corner so they can fight their way out. If you are like me, you can recall when you sped down a freeway or highway to an important appointment at eighty miles an hour, reviewing the proposal or planning the presentation or crunching some final numbers during the harrowing ride. Salespeople are familiar with the concept of "Just in Time."

The worst salespeople rely on this talent. For them, worry is preparation and ad-libbing passes for work. They have taken "winging it" to the level of an art form. They invest minimal time preparing and rely on their power of improvisation to get them through. Sometimes it does, but it often does not, leading to a lack of understanding and control because they have no idea what happened.

Think of a time when you lost an order you believed was a "sure thing." When a sure thing falls through, it's a sure thing that lack of credibility was the issue. Has anyone ever told you that you weren't getting the business because you lacked credibility? Of course not. It's the hidden reason. People in business are much too diplomatic and much too busy to educate salespeople on their lack of professionalism and credibility.

In my research and preparation work to put the Klue game together, I have traveled in the field with several salespeople from each company I work with. I have generally been sent out with top performers. Most are brilliant, but sometimes I have been shocked at what I saw: Salespeople making presentations to a roomful of people without knowing exactly who each person is and why he or she is there. Salespeople plunging into sales presentations without asking questions and exploring the prospect's issues and objectives. Salespeople who have not taken the time to establish their credibility before beginning the sales process.

I attended an appointment with a top sales rep from a company that sells computer networking equipment. We entered the room together and sat down to meet with a group of seven representatives of the prospect's company. The salesperson immediately launched into a very technical presentation, including elaborate diagramming on a white board, of his solution for their company. During his presentation, he focused on his contact and one other man. At one point a woman at the end of the table asked a question in a very soft voice. Without questioning her further, acknowledging her issue, or even looking directly at her, he answered the question and then went on with his technical presentation.

Months later I was working with the company that had been the recipient of the presentation and had an opportunity to talk with several of the company's representatives. I was able to verify my intuitive conclusion: The woman who had been brushed off was a key decision maker. The sales rep did not get the business. The representatives acknowledged that technically he really knew his stuff, but he had not done his homework.

The "Show Up and Throw Up" Presentation

A "show up and throw up" presentation, according to a salesperson I know, is walking into a room cold, with little investigation or preparation, and overwhelming the prospects with your superior product knowledge and awesome technical expertise. You know what? It just doesn't work anymore.

An article in the August 1996 issue of *Sales & Marketing Management* discusses a survey of 418 purchasing managers. Although 68 percent rate salespeople's product and technical knowledge as above average, 72 percent claim that salespeople's familiarity with their companies' business and products is either average, low, or very low. Here are several specific comments from purchasing managers:

> I have many salespeople who come into my office without any knowledge about my business or products. They talk at length about their own products and then just want to make a quick sale, no matter how they get it.

> It's hard to hold good business conversations with them because they often don't know enough about how my company operates.

> They talk too much about themselves, without telling me how they can help my business.

The biggest concern, according to those at companies who hire me, is that they cannot move their salespeople past an obsession with product features and technical presentations. Salespeople resist attempts to shift the focus to customer needs and business issues. And the more technically gifted the salesperson, the greater the resistance. This dilemma is considered so critical by many top corporations that I regularly hear these frightening words: "Maybe we need a new sales force."

New sales force, indeed! Salespeople need to open their eyes to business realities in the 90s. Anyone who does not contribute to the bottom line loses his job. This includes our customers, who require our understanding of the business and financial issues they grapple with. If their focus is reducing cycle times, talk cycle times. If their focus is on increasing employee productivity, talk productivity.

The Solution Is Preparation

Why would salespeople stubbornly cling to features and benefits selling, and resist the focus that customers demand? Because they already know about their product or service; communicating this information is easy and comfortable for them. To discover the customer's needs and objectives requires *work.*

But doing this *work* will get your customer's attention. The fastest and best way to establish credibility and trust is to invest the time required to prepare—period. No shortcuts here. It requires hours and hours of preparation, including researching the company, its business model, its financial structure, and its issues and objectives. Research every key player to discover each one's needs and motives. Prepare for every conceivable question, issue, or outcome. Spend time visualizing the presentation process and follow-up activities, and design a response to everything. *Then use your exceptional talent at improvisation to address the issues and questions you could not possibly have imagined.*

Preparation is hard work. Nolan Ryan, the baseball great, once said, "Pitching is easy. Preparation is hard." This baseball truth is also true in the sales profession. Selling is easy. Preparing to sell is hard work!

Preparing to sell using Visionary Selling skills *requires* this investment of time spent researching your prospect. Some of this research will be valuable, and some will have very little merit. Unfortunately, it is impossible to know in advance which is which. As Lord Leverhulme complained about advertising, "Half the money I spend on advertising is wasted, and the trouble is I don't know which half." Half of the time you spend preparing will be wasted, but there is no way of knowing which information is unnecessary, which objections or issues will never arise, and which of your ideas will miss the mark.

Many baseball players swing two bats before they approach the plate to play. The reason? When they get up to bat, swinging with one bat is easy. They overprepare. Then when their moment comes, they have power to spare. By overpreparing for your presentation, you will have power to spare. And your customers and prospects will feel it.

Create a timetable of the steps required to research a new prospect, such as the thirty-day checklist at the end of this book. Break it down into manageable chunks. Assign a completion date for each step and then stick to it.

What Do They Say About You After You've Left?

There is no difference between what you sell and who you are. In your customer's mind, the two are intertwined. You are your best brochure. What do they say about *you* after you've left?

I recently met with a real estate agent when I considered listing my home. She began by explaining that she had kept her maiden name after her divorce because she could not afford the $300 to appear in court to change it. This revelation didn't exactly foster my confidence in her professional ability. She could not get her calculator to work and didn't have a spare. What if I had been a buyer ready to make an offer? She added her 6 percent sales commission onto the listing price without even discussing it with me. When I asked what she felt was essential to sell my home, she responded, "Price, price, price." I realized that by subtracting her commission I could offer a very low price, price, price. Zero credibility. Did I tell her? No, I did not. Remember, it's the hidden reason.

When you meet with a new prospect, what is your credibility? Zero or ten? Many salespeople assume it is ten, since they haven't done anything wrong yet. It is actually zero. You haven't done anything right yet, either. Don't assume it. Establish it. It is far too important to leave to chance.

Nothing establishes credibility more than your willingness to invest significant time and energy researching the prospect's company, current needs, and vision for the future. It establishes you as a true sales professional. It also creates a resource you can leverage: The time you have invested in research combined with the time they have spent educating you is of value to them.

Think of your relationship with your doctor. On the first visit you spent fifteen minutes filling out forms and another fifteen getting acquainted. On every subsequent visit, vital signs were monitored and noted, and a history was accumulated. This results in a high level of loyalty. You are not likely to change doctors because of a minor issue, such as being kept waiting naked in a freezing office for twenty minutes (besides, they all do that). You have made an investment in the relationship, and that investment creates value.

Your customers will feel the same loyalty to you. They are flattered by your willingness and eagerness to get to know them. They attach value to the time they've spent educating you. Your inside knowledge of who they are and where they are going gives you an inside edge!

Go the extra mile; it's never crowded. It is easy to be more prepared than the competition. It takes very little to outperform them! On a sales call I often mention an increase in the company's stock price or mention its latest product and ask how it is doing in the market. In the next words from the prospect, I can hear the increase in their opinion of me.

It has never been easier to collect this information. You can access a company on the Internet and know plenty about them in ten minutes. Companies share key information on their direction and strategy in annual reports, 10Ks, and business articles. The change in corporate structure from rigid hierarchy to open system means information is more available, and your prospects are more willing to share it with you. Ask them! They are hoping you will ask questions and listen as they tell you who they are.

The Internal Sale

If you are like me, or if your company is like some I've worked for, you heard a nagging voice as you read the story of Leo Rivera's efforts with Eastman Kodak: How did she get the support of Silicon Graphics' management to put that together? She had to obtain the Magic Bus, convert equipment, get several members of the management team to invest significant time—to say nothing of budgetary issues.

It's a good question. Can Visionary Selling be achieved by a salesperson working alone, without considerable management support? Of course, but it will be twice as difficult and only half as effective. So how do you gain the support and assistance of your company's top management to embark on a process that is complex and time consuming, and may not yield results for a considerable period of time? Before you go after the external sale, how do you achieve the internal sale?

From my research it is clear that the salespeople who are most successful in selling to executives and establishing strategic relationships with the "C" level work for companies with a commitment to this process from top management. Are your company's executives currently involved with customers and prospects? If not, how can you initiate this activity? Design a strategy to convince your executives of the importance of meeting with customers to identify needs and objectives, and the benefits of getting personally involved in the sales process.

Top-performing companies such as 3M, Procter & Gamble,

Xerox, Hewlett-Packard, and Owens Corning have implemented programs to increase value to customers through high-level interaction and strategic alliance. Top executive support and participation provide a cornerstone for these programs.

Search for articles in the business press that describe sales successes with executive involvement. Send a copy of the article to the executives of your company, with a note that you would love to discuss the article's merits.

What is so important about establishing an executive interface? Top executives can open doors and build relationships at higher levels. They can help salespeople get into places they normally could not access. The customer feels connected to someone with inside knowledge and strategic pull. Perhaps most valuable, the customer has an ally who is looking out for them long term and doesn't care about what is going to be installed at the end of this month.

Hewlett-Packard's Assigned Executive Program matches every executive, including CEO Lewis Platt, with a specific account to call on and be accountable for. Keith Goodwin, general manager of Computer Systems Organization Americas sales and marketing, says HP does not encourage salespeople to call on the CEO by themselves. Developing executive-level relationships is a team effort, and the Assigned Executive Program assists the salesperson in gaining entry through a peer-to-peer interaction. However, salespeople are calling higher in the organization than before and are focusing on a value-added solution sell rather than a product sell. Keith feels that as HP's products become more of a commodity, adding value through solutions will gain urgency to become a "burning platform."

With Xerox's Focused Executive Program, every executive from the CEO down is involved in one to three accounts. One component is the use of "non-disclosure trips" where key people and senior executives discuss and demonstrate future products with prospects and customers. They expose them to their R&D and then problem-solve and strategize together.

> Identify a member of your company's executive team for one of your high-potential prospects. Design a strategy to connect your executive with an executive in the prospect company, where an alignment of focus or interests or objectives is likely to occur.

3M summarizes their Corporate Strategic Accounts Program with the words "Mutual possibilities—mutual benefits." This program is 3M's focal point in building extraordinary customer relationships to achieve aggressive long-term growth expectations and their vision to become the most innovative enterprise and the preferred supplier.

The program is based on the belief that ongoing teamwork between the companies—at every level—creates powerful relationships that can break through traditional market and technological barriers and open mutual growth opportunities. Two specific aspects of this program are critical to the Visionary Selling process:

1. The salesperson as advocate: 3M assigns a salesperson to the role of strategic accounts manager. The manager's role is to focus on the customer's company and to become an advocate for the customer within 3M. The manager manages a team that provides momentum, resources, inter- and intra-company linkages, technical expertise, and strategic planning power.

2. Function-to-function relationships: 3M people in functional areas such as research and development, sales and marketing, customer service, logistics, technical services, and

information technology talk regularly with their counterparts in the customer company. These major linkages generate market opportunities for both companies.

Owens Corning clearly defines customer strategy and goals by focusing on these three vital areas:

1. True understanding of the customer's business, markets, competitors, and strategies.
2. The customer's expectations and definition of "winning." Jerry Oleshansky claims they literally ask the customer, "What is winning for you?"
3. Internal resources required to meet the customer's needs.

Assembling the Team

James Sheehy, director of executive development at Landmark Graphics, claims that sales today requires an ability to manage multidisciplinary account teams—finance, marketing, pre-sales, and customer support. You must leverage your corporate resources and pull together an association of unrelated groups and have them act as one to enable a "C" level vision.

How? Mike Newman of 3M claims you must first prove the worth of enabling the customer's vision inside your own company. He describes himself as an external advocate for 3M and an internal advocate for the companies he sponsors. He represents their interests to different units and departments of 3M. The question he uses to focus his activity is "How can we help you grow your business, and grow our business at the same time?"

Strive to demonstrate clearly to your customers that you are the most visible member of an entire team of people working on their behalf. Communicate to them that your entire company is focused on improving their business. How? By referring to others in your company, by name and with specific details of how they contributed or their area of expertise. By taking key people with you on as many appointments as possible, from the beginning of the preparation process through implementation and beyond. By connecting others on their team to others on your team. By bringing customers to your site to learn more about you.

Xerox takes this all the way. As winner of the Malcolm Baldridge Award, Xerox opens its doors and shares its "best practices" with customers and prospects so they can learn from the areas where Xerox is exemplary. They provide information for competitive benchmarking, allow prospects to learn from their manufacturing, and share information and ideas in areas that have nothing to do with what they are marketing to the prospect. What kind of message does it send when you offer value that goes beyond what you are selling?

Mike Milligan, senior vice president of customer business development at Procter & Gamble, has implemented a process to align with customers to help them improve sales, market share, and profitability. P&G uses "teams" of account executives with multiskilled capabilities from such diverse areas as finance, information systems, customer service, logistics, and marketing to help them develop systemic long-term relationships. In addressing the National Account Management Association, Mike said, "You are the person best placed to represent both the needs of your company and those of your customers, and you are the person who must join them up."

Build strong relationships with executives within your company and within your prospect's company, and you will become the catalyst for strategic alliances and shared value between them.

Twelve Surefire Ways to Build Credibility

1. Understand their industry and current industry issues.
2. Infiltrate and investigate every aspect of their organization.

3. Align with the "real" vision of the company.
4. Admire and respect who they are.
5. Invest creative thought into improving their business.
6. Gain understanding of the dynamics of their "team."
7. Become an ally of every individual on the team.
8. Take everyone's name just as seriously as you take the decision maker's. (first, spelling of first, last, spelling of last)
9. Have every proposal reviewed by five to ten people in your organization.
10. Take responsibility for everyone in your company who serves your customer.
11. Acknowledge everyone in your company who serves your customer.
12. Do whatever it takes to get your company to honor its promises.

PART III

THE THREE P'S

CHAPTER 7

Prepare

Visionary Selling will position you above the crowd in your understanding of business issues and trends, and over the top in the specific application of your keen intelligence and insight to your prospect's vision of the future. But first you have some work to do.

Two vital components of the Visionary Selling preparation process will achieve these benefits:

1. Information is a strategic asset: Extensive research must be undertaken into your prospect's industry and company so every aspect of your communication is relevant to the prospect's issues and objectives.
2. The visionary in you must be developed: Knowledge of trends and the application of creative thought will lead to value creation through information and ideas that will enhance the business of your prospect.

Vital Component: Information Is a Strategic Asset

You must learn as much as possible about your customer. Considerable work is necessary to obtain and assemble this information, but investing the time and energy required for this level of preparation will provide you with an unbeatable competitive advantage. Learning about the industry and market, and about the specific issues and objectives within that industry and market, prepares the way for valuable ideas and innovative insights that will help your customer's business grow and prosper.

The first step in the preparation process is to research the industry and company of your customer. This can be done at the library, online, or both.

Identify Industry Issues

To assist a customer with challenging issues, you need in-depth knowledge of the customer's industry. The good news is that these issues are common across companies in an industry, and the knowledge you develop for one customer can be used for other companies in the same industry.

Begin by scanning the trade press that relates to the business. If you are not sure which publications are important, you can consult the *Journal of Trade Journals* at the library. Be on the lookout for articles pertinent to the customer's industry or markets in *The Wall Street Journal* and business magazines.

As you read, keep a pile of index cards and Post-its handy. Every time you come across a key business issue, write it at the top of an index card. Carry these in your daily planner. You will find yourself thinking of clever solutions and creative approaches. When you discover a fabulous quote, particularly one that connects with your industry or your market, write it on a Post-it. Keep these pasted on the dashboard of your car or in some other visible spot until you begin to insert them into sales presentations and business conversations regularly.

By the way, I'm not talking about quotes from Howard Stern, Oprah Winfrey, or Dilbert (okay, Dilbert may qualify). Who are the opinion leaders in your customer's business? What are the key economic and political issues affecting that industry, and who is impacting decisions on these issues?

The following matrix is helpful in summarizing key issues by industry. Add other issues as you discover them, or create one for the industry or industries you specialize in.

HEALTH CARE

Sample of Issues

Cost controls
Managed care
Health maintenance organizations (HMOs)
Medicare reimbursement
Purchasing groups replacing medical personnel in buying decisions
Genetic compounds replacing traditional drugs
Congressional debate on health care reform
Drugs approaching end-of-patent period and facing competition from generics

Quotes

"The pharmaceutical industry is at the center of complex relationships between science and society, between business and the public health."

James Flanigan, *Los Angeles Times*

"Health care fraud and abuse currently consume an estimated 10 percent of U.S. health care spending."

Senator Nancy Kassebaum

TECHNOLOGY

Sample of Issues

Convergence of computers, telecommunications, cable, and entertainment industries
Mergers and acquisitions
Impact of Windows 95 and Windows NT
Economic and social impact of the Internet and online services
Global Billings Report (replaced book-to-bill ratio as leading indicator)
Data warehousing and data mining
Home-based and virtual offices
Groupware
Trends in U.S. corporate spending to upgrade equipment
Deregulation of telecommunications and cable industries

Concern about the "Year 2000 problem" in computer databases
Direct broadcast satellite TV and digital TV set-top boxes

Quotes

"The reengineering movement is likely to remain one of the top concerns of CIOs."

Deloitte & Touche survey of 400 CIOs

"The fundamental error that most companies commit when they look at technology is to view it through the lens of their existing processes."

Michael Hammer,
Reengineering the Corporation

FINANCE, REAL ESTATE

Sample of Issues

Estimates of gross domestic product
Federal Reserve Board's assessment of inflation
Interest rates
Global markets
Probability of establishment of monetary union in Europe (EMU)

Quotes

"New technology is creating 'footloose' companies that no longer need to be based in high-cost, highly congested city areas."

Congressional Report: "The Technological Reshaping of Metropolitan America"

CONSUMER PRODUCTS

Sample of Issues

Population and demographic trends
Success of superstores
Focus on value and price
Demand for customization in products and services
Online shopping and marketing on the Internet

Quotes

"The well-informed and demanding new breed of consumer is one of the major factors driving the changes that are rocking corporate America. They have high expectations in quality, service, design—and they want low cost."

Ian Morrison, President, Institute for the Future

TELECOMMUNICATIONS

Sample of Issues

Convergence of computers, telecommunications, cable and entertainment industries
Mergers and Acquisitions
Global telecommunications market
Wireless communications
Telecommunications Reform Bill
Erosion of profit margin on long-distance services

Quotes

"To provide for a pro-competitive deregulatory national policy framework designed to accelerate rapid private-sector deployment of advanced telecommunications and information technologies . . . by opening all telecommunications markets to competition."

Telecommunications Reform Act of 1996

"By the year 2000, the Internet will have reached maturity and become the dial tone of the data communications world."

David Smith, Gartner analyst

Investigating a Specific Company

Never, never, never call on the "C" level of the corporation until you know exactly who the company is and what it does. In Visionary Selling, your unique selling proposition is *specificity.*

What is a unique selling proposition (USP)? It is a concept from the world of advertising that defines what you offer and your competition does not, what you do better than anyone else does, your core competency!

In Visionary Selling, your value lies in the fact that you know more about your prospect or customer than any of your competitors—and even more than many of their own employees! Your goal is to understand their business models and unique characteristics so well that your customer will wonder when you worked for the company.

Nothing is more insulting to a high-level executive or any busy business person than a generic sales call. A few months ago I received a telephone solicitation. I like to get these calls because they give me many examples of what not to do. This salesperson began by saying, "I suppose your business is a lot like mine." "What business am I in?" I asked. She had no idea. How preposterous, to imagine my business was a lot like hers without identifying what business it was. She insulted my intelligence and instantly eliminated any possibility of a business relationship.

> Duplicate a copy of an article mentioning the prospect's company in the trade press. In the margin write a brief idea or suggestion on how to resolve the issue or capitalize on the opportunity.

So how can you discover everything you need to know? Great news: The "C" level vision is published. The vision of the top executives in a public corporation is available to shareholders, the media, and anyone who cares to investigate. This information, which is vital for you to establish an alliance with them, is there for the asking.

What if the company you are targeting is a small business or a private business? The company may still have information, such as published articles or marketing brochures, that will help you discover who they are and what they do.

Small papers, such as the local business journal, often provide insightful, in-depth interviews with executives of corporations in their geographical area. If you are researching a particular individual and cannot find the information you need, why not call your local business journal and suggest the person as the subject of an article or interview? If the journal balks at sending a reporter out, offer to conduct the interview yourself and furnish the information to them for a write-up. This is a brilliant method for establishing personal relationships with executives and with the media.

Go to the Library and Look Up the Company on Infotrac

Infotrac is a computerized database for researching business, management, finance, trade, and investment topics. It contains listings for more than 150,000 companies, including investment analysts' reports on major companies and industries. The *Magazine Index Plus* contains citations, abstracts, and some full text from over four hundred popular and general interest publications. The *National Newspaper Index* contains citations from five major newspapers, including *The Wall Street Journal, Los Angeles Times, The New York Times,* and *The Washington Post.* Infotrac provides a wealth of information and is an ideal place to begin your search.

Select the "General Business File" and enter the name of the company you wish to research. If numerous listings appear, choose the one designated "Corporate." When the public company listing appears, this is what you will find:

Corporation name
Business
SIC codes

Annual sales
Employees
Sales/employees
Year founded
Fiscal year
Features (that is, importer, public stand-alone company, subsidiary, headquarters location)
Stock exchange/ticker
Officers
Subsidiaries
Update date

Print this information (by pressing P on most systems) since it contains an abundance of valuable material. These are just a few of the important items you will discover:

- Business: exactly what the company does, in very specific detail
- Annual sales: the size of the business in gross revenues
- Sales/employees: whether the company is above or below the industry average and whether the trend is up or down for this company
- Fiscal Year: whether the company is currently at the beginning or end of its budgetary year
- Stock exchange/ticker: a review of the stock fluctuations over the last year on *Value Line;* whether the stock is trending up or down; the stock price
- Officers: usually the CEO and CFO are listed and sometimes as many as ten executive officers.

Continue to scan the entire file if you have time. I don't want to mislead you; this is not necessarily easy. Infotrac is a Unix-based system, and it can be tricky to master. If you are used to a Windows-based PC or a Macintosh, you will find it complex and unwieldy. Just take your time, and you will learn plenty about the company you are exploring and eventually master the Infotrac system.

After reviewing the company information screen, scan articles on the company. Make note of the date of the articles at the bottom of the citation; discontinue scanning when you get to articles over a year old, or a few months if you are researching a company in a fast-paced industry. Make note of the number of articles in each category. For example, articles for a high-technology corporation were in these quantities:

Earnings	18
Management	4
Operations	4
Product	45
Sales and Marketing	16

You can draw your own conclusions from the information you receive. The articles are generally indicative of the company's emphasis, since they are often generated from press releases submitted by the company. From the above information I conclude that this company is focused primarily on its product line. Its products are the most important area for me to understand as I begin my alliance with them.

In addition to the information listed, I discovered the following about an electronic computer and prepackaged software company in thirty minutes:

- key philosophies and educational/professional background of the CEO
- it achieved the number one ranking in a survey done by *Dataquest* magazine
- the names, release dates, and descriptions of its top three products

- the details of an industry analysis of its newest product, including price and first shipping date
- its strategy for product line, including a past misstep and its current focus
- material on a competitive analysis

In fifteen minutes I learned the following about a biotechnology company:

- Its two most profitable drugs are maturing in the marketplace.
- Its new drugs will probably not add to earnings until 1998.
- It is counting on mergers to expand its product line.
- It has appointed a top merger lawyer as senior vice president of finance.

Conduct an Online Search

If you prefer to conduct your research online, you have many options. My personal favorite is Hoover's Online Capsule reports (http://www.hoovers.com), which are free. They list company profiles on about ten thousand public and emerging private firms and include contact information, latest sales and filings with the SEC (Securities and Exchange Commission), a listing of senior executives, and a brief business description. If you subscribe, you can review in-depth reports on the twenty-two hundred firms it deems most influential.

From Hoover's you can often jump to the World Wide Web home page of the company you are researching. In a dynamic, interactive format you can research their financials, product information, history, current press releases, and, most important, information on the company executives.

How valuable is this? Before a recent sales appointment, I explored the company's home page. A single mouse click on the blue icon labeled "Executive Team" revealed a list of the top corporate executives with a picture and extensive biographical information for each. I saw the face of the man I was meeting later that week and learned that he had worked eleven years for a company that is one of my best clients. You be the judge.

> Choose a tag line from the prospect's annual report or Web site and use it creatively in your cover letter. Example: As you move the information that moves a customer's world (Adaptec's tag line), your sales team must understand what it is a customer is moving toward (the benefit of Visionary Selling).

Here is another example. One of my clients, Sybase, has a great home page that includes "Presentations on the Web" under its company information. You can download PowerPoint presentations by Sybase executives! Here are a few of the choices, which are constantly updated:

Robert Epstein: Putting the Web to Work
Mark Hoffman: Making Information Systems Paradigm-Proof: The Key to IT Success
Michael H. Forster: Data Warehousing for the 21st Century

If you do not have access to the Internet and want to explore this valuable resource, free Internet access is available in a growing number of communities through libraries and universities.

Steps to Research a Company on America Online

If you are new to online research, this is an opportunity to practice the art of patience. I use America Online, because I can tolerate the frequent bottlenecks and delays as they add new art. At least I can maneuver my way around enough to have something at the end of the session. You will also have an opportunity to practice the skill of focus, since without it you will sign off with absolutely zero information about your prospect. (However, you will have roamed the Library of Congress, planned an impulsive trip to New Orleans, and gotten a low-fat recipe for tiramisu.)

Here are some initial instructions for researching a company on America Online.

1. Go to the *Main Menu*
2. Choose *Reference Desk*
3. Choose *Business & Personal Finance*
4. Choose *Company Research*
5. Choose either *Wall St* or *Hoovers:* Information on each below.

Wall St	**Hoovers**
Company Profiles	Type in company name or ticker symbol, or browse the corporate Web register

Company News
Retrieves from 30-day archive (Reuters, PR News Wire, Business Wire)

Business News
Business Week daily briefing
News listed by industry
New York Times Business News

Live Charts
Contains current stock charts for the Dow Jones Industrial Average, Standard & Poor's 500, and on specific companies

Web Pages
Each is different. The basic ones will show company name, address, and phone/fax/Web site address, names of top officers, fiscal year, annual sales, sales change, number of employees, ticker symbol, and industry. Most provide options such as company profile, quar-

terly financials, and stock chart. Most describe their products or services, and some show their products in full graphic detail. Many contain information about their philosophies. Some are absolutely outrageous and will give you the inside scoop on who they are.

Print the screens or record the information you need. At this point, with less than one hour invested, you will probably be more knowledgeable than 75 percent of the salespeople who call on the company—and possibly half of the employees who work for the company!

Obtain Information from the Company

One of the most positive trends to emerge from business process reengineering is the commitment of companies to define a vision that guides their activities and drives their performance. Large corporations have also become more open and candid in sharing their vision. Ted Pincus, chairman of the nation's largest investor-relations agency, the Financial Relations Board, claims, "We've tried with increasing success to convince companies that saying 'we stand on our record' is never good enough. They've learned that they must share their vision of tomorrow, their hopes and dreams, not as a promise but as a blueprint open for inspection, which they can fine-tune in public as conditions change."

To obtain an annual report, call corporate headquarters and ask for "investor relations." When you ask for a copy, they will not grill you or question your motives. They will assume you are interested in buying stock in the company, which you certainly may be after you become involved in your research. Sometimes you will get voice mail; if so, simply leave a message asking for the annual report and provide your name and address.

You can also ask for recent articles published on the company or that profile its top executives. Magazine articles and newspaper features provide a wealth of information. They give insight into what makes the company tick, not just a cold analysis and statistics on a page. Articles and features based on the "C" level provide a glimpse into how these individuals think and feel. After reading several articles, you will begin to empathize with them.

When I call to ask for the text of executive speeches, my call is sometimes transferred to "public relations." These are the nicest people in the company. Tell them what you're looking for and explore with them what is available. On a recent call I was told the CEO spoke extemporaneously and never utilized a script. They had a videotape available, however, that featured his speech to a large group of CIOs attending the company's users group meeting. In my world, this is a 10++. A copy of the video was made and sent to me. Remember, when you *ask* you *get*.

> Extract quotes from the CEO's speech and refer to them in your cover letter and proposal.

EXTRACT VISION, VALUES, AND CORE COMPETENCIES

Vision

Also known as the mission statement, the vision identifies the very essence of the company. A vision that touches the hearts and minds of the corporation's employees is invaluable. A good vision provides direction, energy, and inspiration. It should identify "who the company is and where it is going."

In their 1993 book *Reengineering the Corporation,* Michael Hammer and James Champy say that a "vision statement, by that or any other name, is the way a company's management communicates a sense of the kind of organization the company needs to become. It describes how the company is going to operate and outlines the kind of results it must achieve."

The most successful corporate executives today are those who understand that their primary mandate is leading the charge for the vision. The future success or failure of corporate America begins with these powerful, courageous, and often charismatic individuals who can formulate a compelling vision of the future, communicate it with energy and enthusiasm among hundreds or thousands of employees, and continuously renew the commitment and passion required to achieve the vision.

The corporate vision often describes a goal that resides somewhere between unlikely and insane. In *Adhocracy,* Robert H. Waterman, Jr., states, "The best teams seem to be driven by big ideas and targets that seem impossible. Big targets create a sense of adventure that attracts the best people in the organization. Impossible goals force people to forget old we-they boundaries and pull together. The purpose, not the box on the chart, becomes the organizing principle. Big ideas force rethinking of old systems." He calls this phenomenon adventure capital.

Do you remember John F. Kennedy's vision statement for the United States of America? "We will take a man to the moon and return him to earth safely by the end of the decade. We do it, not because it is easy, but because it is hard." An entire nation was inspired by these words. More than thirty years later we can still hear them resonating in President Kennedy's strong, dramatic voice.

In *Built to Last,* James C. Collins and Jerry I. Porras explore eighteen companies that have significantly outperformed a close competitor by harnessing the power of a vision. These companies understand that meaning and purpose give emotional energy and spiritual value to their work. The authors illustrate with examples of Disney, a company dedicated to the business of shaping the imaginative life of children and celebrating American values, and Merck, which has always remembered that "the medicine is for the people. It is not for the profits."

The authors claim that these vision statements encourage exceptional companies to tackle BHAGs: Big Hairy Audacious Goals. They claim "a BHAG may be daunting and perhaps risky, but the adventure, excitement, and challenge of it grabs people in the gut, gets their juices flowing, and creates immense forward momentum."

Not All Visions Are Meaningful or Real

Of course, these descriptions reflect an ideal definition of a vision or mission statement. In reality, they are often bland recitations, hypocritical illusions, or wild hyperbole. A management consultant in Colorado, David E. O'Keeffe, made this statement: "I'm a little negative on vision and vision statements. They tend to be an exercise in futility and are difficult to write and/or articulate." One executive spoke of the Lucite-encased copies of the company vision that sat on each executive's desk; he said they were as inspiring as tombstones. Another corporate executive tells a joke about reading a vision statement to a large group of managers representing many companies. When he asked whose company it belonged to, half the managers in the room raised their hand.

Some of us have had the experience of working for a company where the published mission statement bore absolutely no resemblance to reality. "Our people are our most treasured resource" does not go well with announced massive layoffs.

Does this reduce the effectiveness of connecting with the company's vision? Absolutely not. Just remember that the published vision may be different from the real vision, the spoken vision may be worlds apart from the unspoken vision, and the official leadership of the company may be on a different wavelength from the spiritual leadership.

The best visions are working documents, which are in a constant state of dynamic revision. Chris Turner, Xerox Business Services' "learning person," identifies the value of a flexible vision: "We knew the first piece of our change strategy was to create a shared vision, but I never thought of it as a written vision statement. To me, a vision is an ongoing conversation. It's the way we think, individually and collectively, about the community we're creating. It's the principles of the people in the organization. It's never frozen, it's never set. It's energy or spirit."

Sample Visions

The vision is often found on the flyleaf of the annual report or within the first several pages. The following are some of my personal favorites:

> "We are an organization of dedicated people committed to improving the quality of the lives we touch."
>
> PacifiCare, a large health maintenance organization

> "IC Sensors will be the meanest and baddest micromachining company in the entire universe."
>
> IC Sensors (Milpitas, California)

> "A Coke within arm's reach of everyone on the planet."
>
> The Coca-Cola Company

> "Boundaryless . . . in all our behavior.
> Speed . . . in everything we do.
> Stretch . . . in every target we set."
>
> General Electric Company

> "Worldwide airline of choice."
>
> Delta Air Lines

> "To be recognized as one of the finest bakers in the world.
> To be recognized as a model workplace.
> To maintain a healthy level of profitability.

We will reach our vision by bringing delights to our customers and showing the world a better way."

Just Desserts Inc., a provider of fine baked goods

"Encircle Caterpillar."

Komatsu Ltd., a manufacturer of construction equipment

Greg Steltenpohl is the cofounder and co-CEO of Odwalla, a maker of fresh fruit juices. His description of a vision statement is one I adore: "A vision statement should set an unattainable goal while giving insight into a corporation's values and serving as an inspirational touchstone. A vision statement is like the sun. You can't ever get there, but it's an attractive force that stimulates the growth of many things."

This man is a poet! And sure enough, Odwalla's vision statement is expressed in the form of a poem:

Odwalla
A breath of fresh,
Intoxicating rhythm,
Living flavor,
Soil to soul,
People to planet,
Nourishing the body whole.

The Ultimate Sales Tool

I dare you to tell me that reading these vision statements does not give you some unique, daring, and possibly brilliant ideas for how to sell to these companies. Forget the features of your product or service. Save the solutions for later. Here is your opportunity to connect with them soul to soul. You can capture the essence of who they are and who they are striving to become. You can glimpse a magical world of concepts and emotions that define their corporate identity.

How do you apply the information contained in the vision statement to your product or service? While waiting for an appointment in the stunning, luxurious lobby of Borland's corporate headquarters in Scott's Valley, California, I was admiring their unique chairs, which looked as if they had been woven from bands of shimmering golden wood. The receptionist explained that the lobby design had been done by the Knoll Group in San Francisco, and the chairs were the work of Frank Gehry. She handed me the *Borland Campus User Guide,* which provides information for visitors to the building. The booklet explained the lobby design: "Kevin Roche is dedicated to an architecture that creates space conducive to productivity, yet adds value to the work experience—*qualities that coincide with Borland's vision.*"

You've heard the slogan, "People don't buy because they understand. They buy because they feel understood." This vitally important and critically revealing information is available for the asking. Take it and use it!

Values

Most employees today are seeking a stronger sense of meaning and fulfillment in their work. They want to be involved in a purpose and an endeavor that goes beyond simply collecting a paycheck. They need to believe they are part of an organization that stands for something and is based on a value system which is clear, consistent, and ethical.

An example is AT&T, which has published their values as follows below:

Our Common Bond
We Commit to These Values to Guide
Our Decisions and Behavior:
Respect for Individuals
Dedication to Helping Customers

Highest Standards of Integrity
Innovation
Teamwork

By living these values, AT&T aspires to set a standard of excellence worldwide that will reward our shareowners, our customers, and AT&T people.

In *Built to Last,* authors Collins and Porras discuss William Procter and James Gamble's most significant contribution to the company they built: a spiritual inheritance of deeply ingrained core values transferred to generation after generation of Procter & Gamble people.

Sun Microsystems' founder, Scott McNealy, is building a corporate culture based on his personal motto: Kick butt and have fun. General Electric, one of the best-run companies in the world, continues to improve in performance and profitability with this motto: Find a better way every day.

Oracle Corporation, the world's largest vendor of database software and information management services, demonstrates pride in a characteristic of their people through this vignette in the 1995 annual report: *"We're an incredibly competitive company comprised of incredibly competitive people, and sometimes this competitiveness comes out in ways that make us smile. Last time we had a blood drive, I heard one donor suddenly shout to another in triumph, Beat you! because she had managed to give her pint first."*

Company values are often used to lure the gifted and talented to choose one company over another for employment. Lawrence Ellison, CEO of Oracle, called upon a food service innovator to implement his vision for gourmet cuisine served in an elegant ambiance to fuel his company's drive into the twenty-first century. Obviously, Oracle considers appreciation and enjoyment of good food and fine dining to be a company value.

BSG Corporation is a $65 million computer services company that competes with giant rivals Andersen Consulting and EDS by moving faster than they do. How? They've created a culture where urgency is at the core of everything the company does. How does the value of urgency translate into real life? Imagine this: BSG holds their "annual" meetings every quarter. BSG's CEO, Steven G. Papermaster, claims, "For us, a year's worth of change occurs every quarter. So the need to reinforce our culture and values—as well as focus on business issues—is the equivalent of a year's worth of issues."

Lucent Technologies' corporate symbol is an innovation ring. Hand-drawn in red, it is strikingly unusual from a corporate perspective. "We felt this hand-drawn brush stroke would symbolize the creativity and human energy of Bell Labs. It is circular, never-ending, and also implies an air of unpredictability. Red was chosen because it's the most confident, entrepreneurial color," said Dave Shaver, vice president of advertising for Lucent.

> Make reference to the prospect's values in your presentation, such as: "As a company who is known far and wide for your competitive spirit, you will appreciate the competitive advantage this proposal offers." Contribute to their sense of pride in their company and culture.

Core Competencies

Simply, what does the company do best? The company's core competencies are directly analogous to your greatest strengths as an individual. We all know that the most successful people are those who identify their exceptional talents and then exploit them for all they are worth. Successful corporations are no different. They have come to this conclusion: They do not need to do everything well, but they had better do something especially well. And they need to know what it is and who can benefit.

In *Competing for the Future,* Gary Hamel and C. K. Prahalad define core competencies as a bundle of skills and technologies that enables a company to provide a particular benefit to customers. To be first in the future, they claim a corporation must be able to answer these questions: Given our particular portfolio of competencies, what opportunities are we uniquely positioned to exploit? What can we do that other companies might find difficult to do?

How can you use information on your prospect's core competencies to connect with them? When I accompanied a salesperson from one of my client companies, I saw an effective sales application of this information. The first page of his proposal itemized the prospect's core competencies. The second page talked about his company's core competencies. The third page established a synergy between the two and outlined a mutually beneficial partnership. Although this proposal was not delivered to the "C" level, it was so focused on executive-level issues that it might easily be passed along or gain entry for this salesperson at a later time.

Visionary Selling Applied to Sony Corporation

Pretend for a moment that you have an appointment with Sony Corporation. Imagine the approach you would normally take in meeting with key decision makers and presenting your product or service. Now review the information below on Sony's core ideologies, extracted from *Built to Last* by Collins and Porras, which featured Sony as one of their visionary companies.

- To experience the sheer joy that comes from the advancement, application, and innovation of technology that benefits the general public *(vision)*
- To elevate the Japanese culture and national status *(value)*
- To be a pioneer—not following others but doing the impossible *(core competency)*

Would the change in your presentation style and areas of focus create a stronger bond and alliance with Sony than if you were unaware of this information? Would your understanding of who they are and what they value position you advantageously over the competition?

The annual report should give you a good idea of who they are and where they are going (vision), what they stand for or aspire to be (values), and how they intend to get there (core competencies.)

Additional Information in the Annual Report

As you review the annual report, here are some additional items to focus on:

- Graphs and charts of revenues, earnings per share, and revenue per employee
- Letter from the CEO and president
- Overall visual style and communication tone
- Specific corporate culture references, for example, Disney calls its employees "cast members" and work shifts are referred to as "performances"
- "C" level terminology, such as SBRs (strategic business results), AMP (account management planning), breakthrough objectives, stretch goals, critical success factors, value-stream, integrated solutions

The first half of the annual report, with all the color and pictures, is fun to read. You will discover far more interesting and insightful information in the second half. In fine print and often titled "management discussion and analysis," it contains full disclosure of product strategies, competitive threats, regulatory issues, and so forth. Also examine the 10Q and 10K reports for short-term financial trends. (In 1989 the SEC mandated that trend information be part of every 10Q and 10K report.)

Include the prospect's logo next to your logo on the cover sheet of your proposal.

Vital Component: The Visionary in You Must Be Developed

You've heard the expression "We are drowning in information but starved for knowledge." Our intent is to take this abundance of information and use it as a springboard for innovative thought.

In the last few years I've rediscovered camping as a way to recharge my batteries and restore my spirit. Recently, I was camping under a huge and gnarled oak tree when I was suddenly pelted by an acorn shower. The oak tree periodically shoots out many tiny acorns, which are pointed like an arrow on one end to facilitate their flight and assist their plunge to the earth. Hundreds of these tiny acorns must hit the ground with a thud for just a few to take root and grow into trees.

Think of the creative process as an oak tree. The tiny acorns are ideas. The ground is comprised of your knowledge base, all the information you possess and all the experiences you have had in your life. What can you do to increase your success in sales by shooting off more ideas? How can you prepare fertile ground to receive them and give them life? How can you draw on your resources of intelligence and intuition to assist you?

Right and Left Brain Hemispheres

As you know, your brain is divided into two hemispheres. The left hemisphere is organized, analytical, and logical. Think of it as a Marine sergeant. The right hemisphere is sensory, intuitive, and dynamic. Think of it as a rambunctious four-year-old. These two hemispheres are constantly battling each other for dominance, in a conflict reminiscent of sibling rivalry.

In conducting industry and company research, the left hemisphere of the brain is used. It loves to research, organize, write, and diagram in neat orderly rows. That is why the left brain is responsible for reading, writing, and mathematics, and it takes its work seriously.

The right brain is turned off by these approaches and is most favorably involved when reading and writing are eliminated. It needs to see, hear, touch, and feel. Always on the lookout for sensory pleasures, the right hemisphere of your brain delights in visual extravaganzas: the beauty of art or nature and the impact of color; auditory treats such as music; the tactile stimulation of swimming or massage; and all emotional expressions such as personal conversation and drama. The right brain surges into prominence when we are involved in activities that stimulate our senses, especially if we are relaxed and not striving to achieve a specific outcome.

Have you ever wondered why you get your best ideas in the shower, of all places? No Day-Timer. No cellular phone. No computer. No paper and pencil! Is this some bizarre cosmic joke?

The reason you get your best ideas in the shower or while running or at 4:00 A.M. is that the left brain has taken a rest and the right brain is in its element. As Fritjof Capra, a gifted physicist, explains, "During periods of relaxation after concentrated intellectual activity, the intuitive mind seems to take over and can produce the sudden clarifying insights that give so much joy and delight."

Right Brain Specialty

It is the intuitive mind, or right brain, that we will use to develop the visionary in you. Why? The specialty of the right brain is dynamic, holistic thinking. The right brain can take countless pieces of information and detect the pattern that exists among them, as if by magic. It can find surprising and original connections between different ideas. The right brain specializes in synthesis, synchronicity, and convergence.

The more seemingly disparate and unrelated but key issues and pieces of information we can synthesize into our presentation and proposal, the more unique and captivating it will be. This requires creativity, innovation, and a large dose of non-linear thinking. We want to think what has not been thought before and see things that have not yet been envisioned. Our ultimate goal is to thrust our plethora of information into fertile soil where it will take root and blossom into one or many glorious ideas.

The Quest for a Brilliant Idea

How many truly original ideas have you had in your life? Think of the events preceding their occurrence. Were you engrossed in facts, figures, and information? Were you pushed up against a deadline, frantic and desperate to complete the project in time? Did you finally throw up your hands in frustration, maybe even give up? This is often the state of events that produces original thinking and new ideas. You've heard the cliché: Necessity is the mother of invention.

Why would you want to voluntarily subject yourself to this trauma? Because in the fast-moving and unpredictable world we live in today, individuals who are capable of producing original ideas and novel insights are handsomely rewarded. In the age of computers, the only irreplaceable skill is thinking. The ability with maximum shelf life is creativity.

What steps are required to become more creative and innovative in your ideas and solutions? How do you smash the paradigm in how you perceive your product or service? How do you find a convergence of your customer's objectives, the innovative application of your product or service, and emerging market opportunities?

Five Fun Ways to Light Your Creative Spark

1. EXPOSURE TO OTHER PROFESSIONS, INDUSTRIES, CULTURES, AND LIFESTYLES

A young man once approached Peter Drucker and asked how he could become more creative. Drucker responded, "Learn to play the violin." It may appear that he was ridiculing the young man's query, but the response is actually quite valid. To become more creative and innovative you must expose yourself to new and different ideas, experiences, and approaches.

Here is an effective and enjoyable way to get started. Designate one night a month as "library night." Go to the library, walk up and down the aisles of the magazine section, and select a few magazines you have never read before and normally never would. Sit in a chair and look through each one. Read any articles that appeal to you. Study the columns. Read the letters to the editor. Explore the advertisements. When a mental connection occurs, turn the magazine over in your lap. Let the information or idea "percolate." As Max Dixon of National Speakers Association says, "Just let that idea relax by the fire until it feels like talking." See where it takes you.

By doing this you will expose yourself to industries, professions, cultures, and lifestyles you have never explored before. You will discover new approaches and leading edge ideas from a variety of industries and professions. You will broaden your perspective and your ability to see things from many different angles.

The Internet is a fabulous way to explore a wide range of ideas and perspectives without leaving the comfort of your chair. When you surf the Net, you are traveling through cyberspace with little structure or purpose other than to immerse yourself in visuals and facts that are new to you. Since the entire experience is right-brain oriented, it is an ideal method for stimulating creativity and discovering unusual connections and innovative patterns.

Many breakthroughs are the result of detecting a hidden pattern of connections among things, or juxtaposing elements or ideas that do not ordinarily go together.

For example, "Just in Time" inventory management did not originate in the automobile industry. It began in the grocery business. Excess inventory in the produce, meat, dairy, and bakery departments would rot on the shelves, so it was essential to stock inventory *just in time* for sale. The automobile industry borrowed the concept and reduced the cost of stocking excess inventory. Now JIT is an integral component of the total quality management process used by most manufacturing companies and many other industries as well.

What ideas are being used by other industries and professions that could benefit your customer or prospect? What conceptual insight can you derive from other cultures or lifestyles that will trigger your creative spark, allowing you to see things that haven't been seen before or think things that haven't been thought?

Talk to your own people, especially in customer service, accounting, and operations. They interact with customers at different stages of the process and often receive valuable input about potential improvements or breakthroughs in your product, its application, or other opportunities. They also have a different perspective, which is valuable in generating ideas and suggestions.

2. Explore trends

Visionary Selling requires an understanding of where social, demographic, economic and technological trends are leading and the business developments that will have an impact in the future.

To offer maximum value in Visionary Selling, you must become a trendmaster. According to Faith Popcorn, author of *The Popcorn Report,* "Anticipating a new reality is the beginning of the process of creating it. Tracking the trends is one way to anticipate new realities and help our clients create them."

As you read articles and listen to news shows, look for answers to these questions:

What is the trend?

How will the trend manifest itself in my industry?

What are the implications of this trend for my industry? For my customers and prospects? For manufacturing, finance, sales and marketing, human resources?

How can I integrate information on this trend into my sales strategy?

How can I provide advance warning of this trend to my customers and prospects?

What are the major professional lessons reflected in this trend?

How is this trend likely to evolve in the coming years?

The Strategic Convergence™ diagram below will assist you as you identify and explore the trends and changes affecting your customer or prospect.

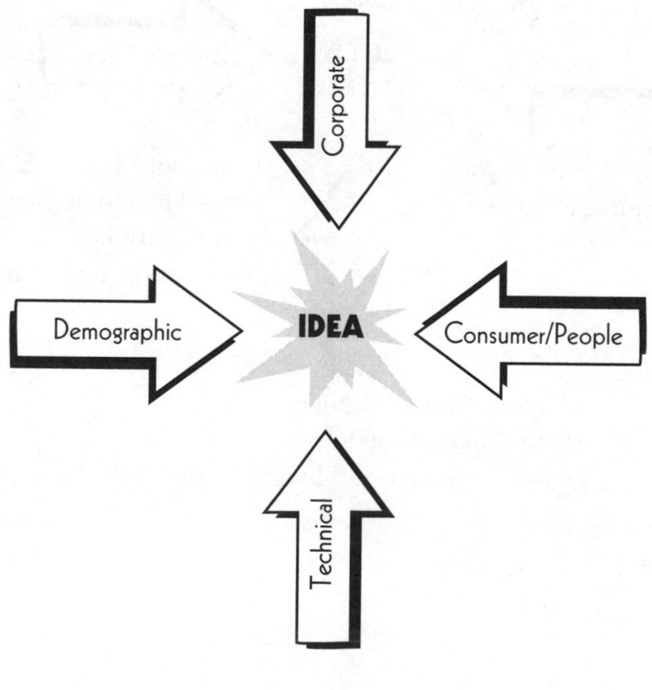

The concepts included in this book were created using this process. As a result of meeting with the "C" level of companies I work with and listening to their current goals and issues, as well as reading the business and trade press, I compiled the following information:

Focus on vision, values, core competencies
Increase in outsourcing (even key functions)
Quest for industry foresight
Interest in futurism

Corporate

Demographic

IDEA

Consumer/People

College-educated sales reps
Buying decision/higher level
Quest for "meaningful" work

Technical

Desire for customization
Move beyond problems to collaboration
Need for connectedness

Rapid pace of change
Information age
Mobile employees linked by networked computers

These are issues affecting all my customers and probably most of yours. This is my backdrop for designing a strategic collaboration for every customer I work with, and then I add specific customer trends, such as business process reengineering (BPR) or competitive threats or recent industry and company mergers.

What if your prospect was a software company looking for new economic opportunities and consumer trends? Scan the information below and formulate an area of potential profit for them. My suggestion is software to manage the complexities of electronic commerce and online banking. What's yours?

Global markets
Focus on short-term results, quarterly earnings
Mobile employees

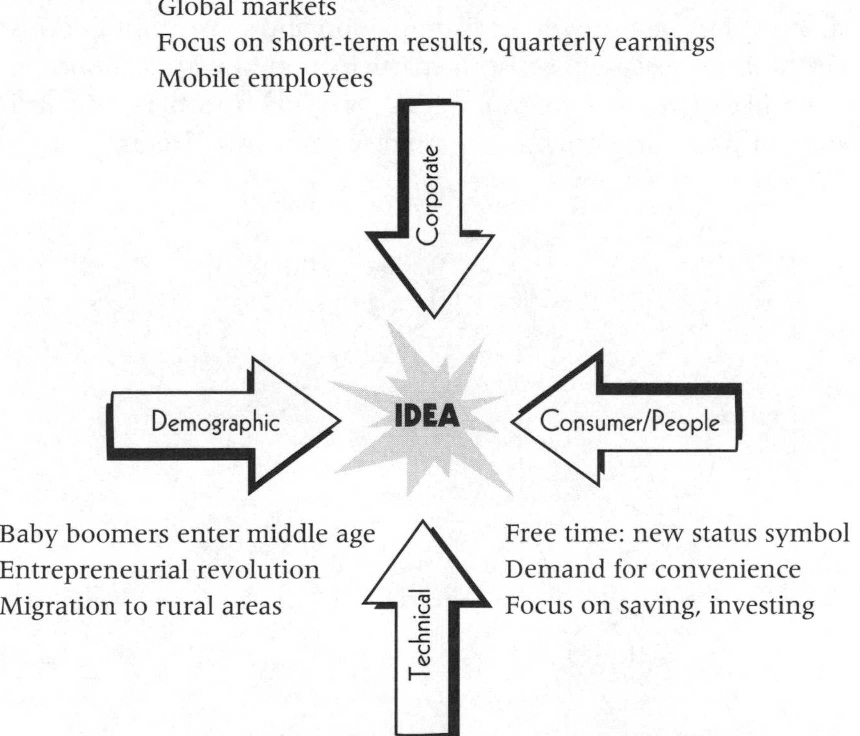

Baby boomers enter middle age
Entrepreneurial revolution
Migration to rural areas

Free time: new status symbol
Demand for convenience
Focus on saving, investing

Internet and online shopping services
Wireless communications
Collaborative computing software; groupware
Data warehousing and data mining

3. Techniques to stimulate creativity

Mindmapping

One technique useful for generating unusual, wild, harebrained, and brilliant ideas is mindmapping. Mindmapping enables you to compile complex issues, significant information, and relevant trends into a format that is non-linear and invokes the right brain to action. The goal is to stimulate rather than strangle the right brain. If you are an artist or like to doodle, sketch rather than write the information. Use different colors of ink. Buy stickers and use them to illustrate possibilities. Remember, anything you can do to increase the sensory stimulation and sense of fun of this part of the process will enlist the participation of your right brain. Being like a small child, your right brain loves to play and will come to your party only if you promise games and treats.

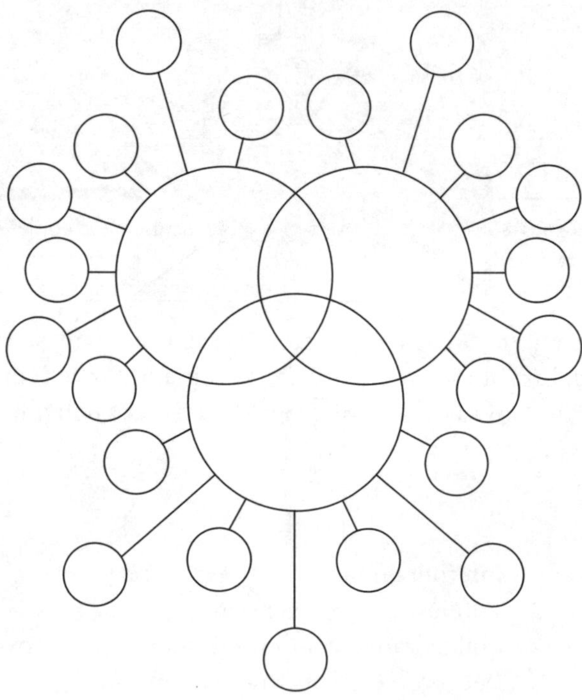

Thirty Ideas

Another approach is to list thirty ideas as quickly as possible. You know how this works. The first ten are easy. The second ten are harder. The last ten almost kill you. And it is the last ten that take you to new ground, unknown and unavailable to your competition who haven't invested this time and focused their creative effort.

Do not judge, censor, or explore these ideas now. This is a right brain activity, and the right brain is very sensitive. If you allow the internal sensor that is your left brain to interfere, the flow of valuable ideas will slow to a mere trickle. As Anita Roddick, president of The Body Shop International, explains, "Creativity comes by breaking the rules, by saying you're in love with the anarchist."

> **Schedule a "free day" with time to process information and reflect. Go somewhere unusual—a train station, a mom-and-pop hardware store, a local library, or a museum.**

4. Future Fantasy

Management guru Peter Drucker claims the best way to predict the future is to create it. The best way for a sales professional to profit from the future is to position himself as someone who understands it.

Imagine that you are standing side by side with your customer at some point in the future. Five years? Ten years? Select a date and put yourself in that place and time. Now look around you. What do you see? What is going on? What is happening in your customer's industry and company?

Now that you have a good grasp of where you are, look back to 1997. What should have been done in 1997 to prepare for the reality you see? What strategies would have maximized the advantage or improved the position of your customer? What actions would have led to great success?

This technique is a personal favorite of Ted Turner. When Ted looked into the future from the vantage point of the late 1970s, he envisioned a fundamental transition. People's lives were becoming more chaotic and less structured. They were working long or odd hours and traveling more. The reality of people working nine to five, arriving home at six to eat dinner and watch the news, was changing. Looking into the future and betting that this trend would continue or increase, he designed a news network based on a future fantasy. CNN would provide the latest news anytime you had a few moments to watch. If you were unavailable at six but eager for news at 7:36, that was just fine with Ted. He created a new paradigm of news coverage to capitalize on an emerging social reality.

Memorize these words of Ted Turner's. They are a blueprint for the successful executive, salesperson, or investor of the future:

> Look into the future and ask: What is the future going to look like? What can I do to be in the right spot at the right time? Once it's obvious to everyone that something is going to be successful, the opportunity is gone. Then anybody can do it!

> Form a "Future Fantasy" group. Choose people from several professions and industries who will get together once a month to brainstorm about the future of business.

5. Catapult to new levels of creative thought

Your awareness of current trends and their impact on business issues is invaluable as a base for creative thought. We are striving, however, to attain new levels in our thought processes. We seek to define and integrate new paradigms into our prospects' and customers' organizations. Our goal is to develop an ability to move past what is common knowledge and accumulate a vast storehouse of uncommon ideas.

Here is a simulated example of the creative process of Visionary Selling at its nerve-jangling, gut-jarring best. At a recent Klue session I conducted with a company that sells client/server development tools, one team had a hypothetical case study that featured J. Edgar "Hoser," the head of the FBI. J. Edgar was a domineering command-and-control, megalomaniac type who had recently been publicly disgraced twice: on *60 Minutes,* where it was revealed that the FBI was hemorrhaging red ink and needed to get in line with the balanced budget amendment, and during a terrorist attack when their antiquated information system failed to alert the field offices in time for an adequate response. The team's mandate was to convince J. Edgar to convert to client/server technology. However, J. Edgar had already thrown them out of his office once for even suggesting he should expose FBI intelligence to "computer hackers and terrorists."

One bold and brave team presented a strategy that recommended putting the FBI's data on the Internet! They would remind J. Edgar that the FBI are experts on security. Everyone is attempting to resolve security issues on the Internet; who better to lead the way than the FBI? At the same time, by using a network that was already in place, the FBI would eliminate the huge capital investment required to design and implement its own client/server network.

This plan would require a lot of additional thought and planning (the team formulated their strategy for this hypothetical situation in twenty minutes), but the seed of possibility is brilliant. This is exactly the type of idea that would get the attention of a man like J. Edgar, who has issues to resolve and must renew his leadership position. A truly controversial, provocative, and counterintuitive idea.

On your quest to create value for your prospect, you have completed research to discover pertinent information and applied creativity to formulate provocative ideas. In the next chapter we will travel one step beyond as we seek convergence between the two.

CHAPTER 8

Package

The goal of Visionary Selling is to package information into a concise presentation that a top executive will want to hear. Andrew Grove, CEO of Intel, advises, "Let chaos reign and then rein in chaos." We must rein in the extensive research and unbridled brilliance of the last chapter to a format that stimulates our comprehension, creativity, and collaboration.

I know salespeople. I am one. Long forms and detailed questionnaires are a turnoff. The simple and adaptable format that follows was designed to assist you in assembling many tidbits of information into a concise, cohesive presentation. After completing it, I suggest you carry it around for a few days and allow ideas to "percolate."

Seeking Strategic Convergence

Remember the "C" level formula: Leverage vision, values, and core competencies to increase profits, power, and position in the future. As you design your presentation, seek convergence among the three vital components below:

1. Vision, values, and core competencies: Who are they? What do they stand for? Where are they going?
2. Your product or service: Who are you? What do you offer? How can you help your customer achieve its objectives or overcome its obstacles? How can you increase your customer's

profits, power, or position in the future? How does your solution align with your customer's vision, values, and core competencies?

3. Trendmaster tips and provocative ideas: What information do you bring that is controversial or counterintuitive? What novel ideas or fresh insights can you offer? How can you create value for your customer's company?

Sample Format for Sun Microsystems

The following was completed using Sun's 1996 annual report, 10K for fiscal year ending June 30, 1996, and a *Business Week* article on CEO Scott McNealy (January 22, 1996.) No "inside information" was included. Before calling on an executive at Sun, I will use this information to design specific, focused questions. During the call I will have this format in front of me to guide and direct the conversation. After the call I will add additional information I have discovered.

Vision, Values, and Core Competencies

Vision: The Network is the Computer. Sun is evangelistic in its dedication to the value of network computing and of open systems, and believes the true value of computers is achieved when they work together in networks.

Values:

- Continual innovation and leadership
- Controversial
- Competitive high jinks (Motto: Kick butt and have fun)

Core Competencies:

Global leader in enterprise network computing

Your Product or Service

Take a moment to think of what you could offer Sun. Is there a fit between your product or service and their vision? Would your product or service support their quest for dominance in network computing? Can you assist them in leveraging their core competencies?

Trendmaster Tips and Provocative Ideas

Review the information below on the issues, trends and developments affecting Sun.

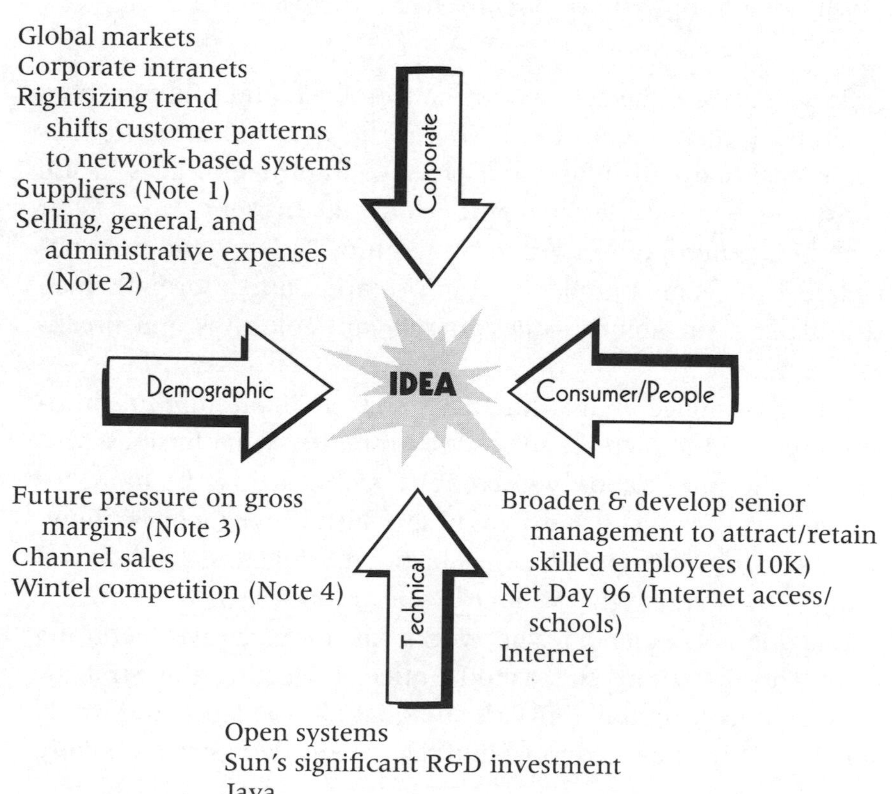

Notes:

1. The company is increasingly dependent on the ability of its suppliers to design, manufacture, and deliver advanced components required for the timely introduction of new products.

2. Selling, general, and administrative expenses increased $293 million, or 20.4 percent, in fiscal 1996.

3. Because Sun operates in a highly competitive industry characterized by increasingly aggressive pricing, systems repricing actions may be initiated in the future; these may result in a downward pressure on gross margin.

4. The Company is facing increasing competition with respect to products based on microprocessors from Intel coupled with operating system software from Microsoft.

As you review the above information, ideas and solutions may begin popping into your head. That is the whole idea. Do not become obsessed with whether a piece of information goes in the consumer or the demographic column. Do not labor over whether something is a vision or a value. The one and only objective is to get an abundance of information into a format which stimulates your ability to design relevant solutions and breakthrough ideas.

I have compiled an assortment of facts in an attempt to stimulate your ability to create solutions, no matter what business you are in. The information you compile will of course be more focused on your industry and areas of specialty. Don't go too far, however. Remember that it is the unusual tidbit or additional insight you bring to the solution that will make your proposal stand out.

Imagine a salesperson who works for an executive recruiting firm. The first thing she would notice, reviewing the Strategic Convergence diagram above, is the goal to broaden and develop senior management to attract and retain skilled employees. Before consulting her Rolodex for potential candidates for Sun, she must consider several other items. Sun is expanding into global markets; therefore, an executive with global expertise or background would have an advantage. Since pressure on margins is an issue, anyone with a successful track record in maintaining profit margins in a competitive market would grab Sun's attention. And what about its culture of "kicking butt and having fun" or its involvement in wiring elementary schools for Internet access? Incorporating information about a potential candidate's personal style or community involvement might produce an unbeatable combination.

Many executive recruiters would like to work with Sun. The one who presents a potential candidate who incorporates valuable background and expertise specifically applicable to three or more of Sun's issues or objectives would get the company's attention. Sun would recognize the fit, but more important, it would recognize that the recruiter understood who the company is and what it needs!

Sample Format for BankAmerica

Vision, Values, and Core Competencies

Vision: Be the most important provider of financial services to customers in our markets by developing deep relationships based on our breadth of high-quality financial products and services and our global capabilities. (*U.S. Corporate and International Banking*)

Values:

- Corporate responsibility and community reinvestment
- Teamwork at every level of the corporation by seeking ways

to eliminate artificial barriers and rewarding people who achieve excellence through teamwork.

Core Competencies:

- Ranked as the nation's leading relationship bank in a recent survey of Fortune 1,000 companies conducted by Goldman Sachs
- Ability to offer a comprehensive range of financial services
- Global network

Your Product or Service

Take a moment to think of what you could offer BankAmerica. Is there a fit between your product or service and their vision? Would your product or service support their quest to consolidate or outsource processing operations or increase efficiency with advanced technology? Can you assist them in leveraging their core competencies?

Trendmaster Tips and Provocative Ideas

Review the information below on the issues, trends and developments affecting BankAmerica.

Imagine you are a salesperson selling database storage and management products. BankAmerica is your top prospect. Consider the following potential linkages between prospect and product.

- BankAmerica intends to be the most important provider of financial services to customers in their markets. Your product would enable BankAmerica to capitalize on existing data in order to design new products based on customers' existing patterns of use.

Investing in "relationship-building businesses"
Client-focused organization
Risk management key determinant to overall financial performance
Banking changes: Competition from non-banks, Congress changing rules, consolidations

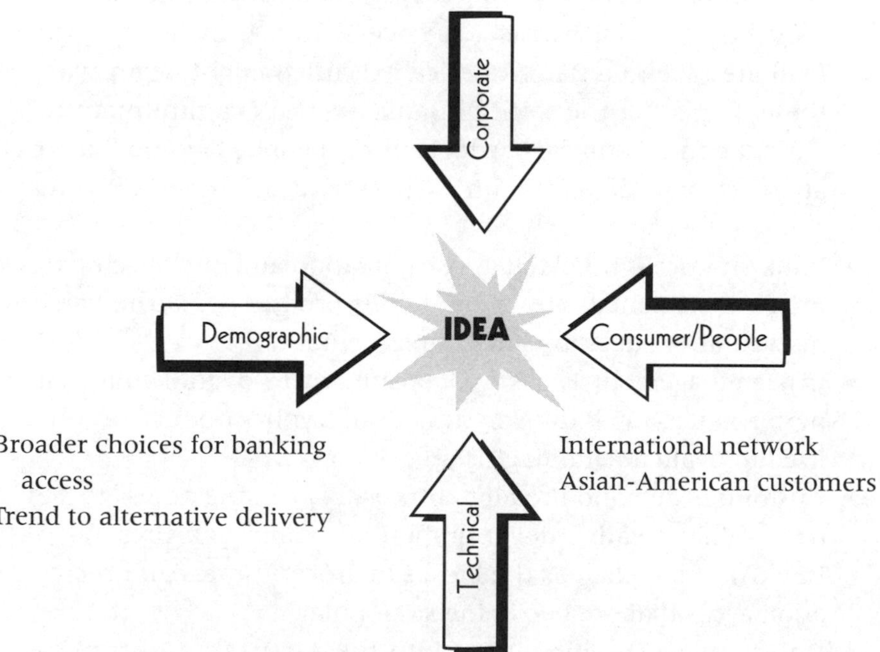

Money management software
BankAmerica's World Wide Web site; first with site on America Online
Interactive banking
Computerized credit scoring

- BankAmerica prefers to deepen customer relationships with their breadth of products. The bank could customize a portfolio of services of interest for each customer.
- BankAmerica's global network could be simplified and stream-

lined with software to manage currency fluctuations and language barriers.

- BankAmerica upholds a value of corporate responsibility and community reinvestment. How does your company approach these issues?
- BankAmerica is highly supportive of teamwork and the removal of artificial barriers. A cover letter, E-mail, or voice mail message to a BankAmerica executive might begin with these words: "In the spirit of BankAmerica's commitment to elimination of artificial barriers among people, I would like to approach you directly with a specific idea I have for your company."
- BankAmerica is involved in consolidation and outsourcing to increase efficiency. How would your product assist the bank in evaluation, decision, and implementation?
- Risk management is a key determinant to overall financial performance for BankAmerica. Could your product be utilized to evaluate and flag risk?
- Customers demand broader choices for banking access these days. What creative delivery methods could you present to BankAmerica, such as the kiosks in grocery stores and recreation areas that are becoming so popular?
- Do you have specific insight into the Asian-American market?
- Could your product interact with their Web site? BankAmerica could offer a quiz or worksheet to determine financial wellbeing or retirement goals. The customer would receive value in free financial advice, and valuable data would assist BankAmerica in future product design and marketing strategies.

Sample Format for 3M

Vision, Values, and Core Competencies

Vision: Accelerating growth through innovation and a sharper focus on customers worldwide. (3M is in the process of a major strategic initiative to become an even stronger company.)

Values:

- Innovation (27 percent of 1995 sales came from new products launched within the last four years)
- Entrepreneurial spirit
- Environmental champion

Core Competencies:

- Sales per employee have increased an average of 7 percent a year over the last five years
- Strong technology base to create innovative solutions to customer needs

Your Product or Service

Take a moment to think of what you could offer 3M. Is there a fit between your product or service and their vision? Would your product or service support their quest for a sharper focus on customers worldwide? Can you assist them in leveraging their core competencies?

Trendmaster Tips and Provocative Ideas

Review the information below on the issues, trends, and developments affecting 3M.

Markets products in 200 nations
Breast implant litigation
Launching data storage/imaging businesses as independent company
Goal to become "faster, stronger, more focused"
Simplifying business processes to make it easier for customers

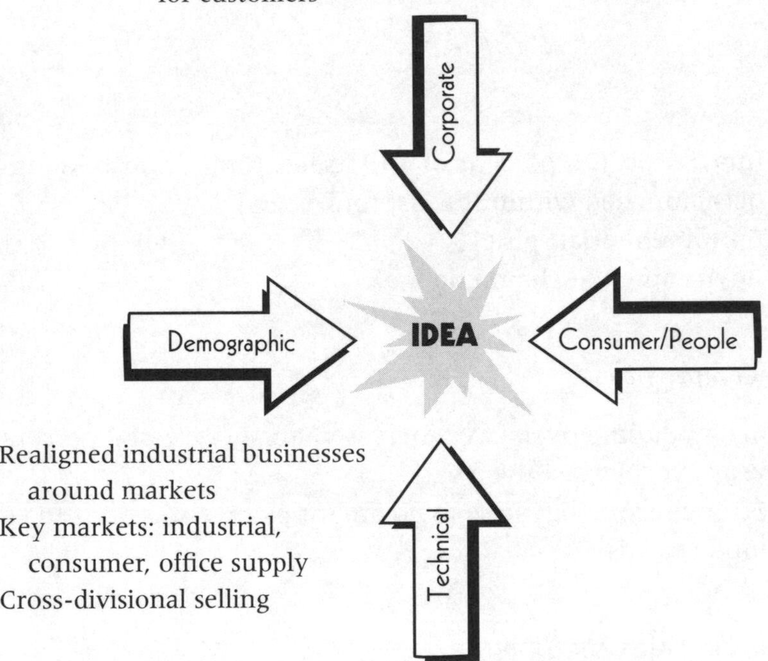

Realigned industrial businesses around markets
Key markets: industrial, consumer, office supply
Cross-divisional selling

History of developing products that "change the basis of competition"
Microreplication (breakthrough in materials science)

Let's imagine a person who markets financial services is designing an action plan to follow in order to align with 3M. The person must do the following:

- Discover more about the major strategic initiative and potential opportunities for application of financial services.

- Discover more about the spinoff of the new company.
- Explore risk management; many of 3M's products are used by the dental, medical, manufacturing, automotive, and safety industries, and the company is currently involved in litigation.
- Mention his company's history of developing products that "change the basis of competition."
- Present his company's global expertise.
- Develop several key ideas on how new, innovative financial services could help 3M become faster, stronger, and more focused.
- Develop several key ideas on how improved financial services would assist with 3M's goal of simplifying business processes.
- Share information and expertise about the industrial market, which his company specializes in.

Sample Format for Amgen

VISION, VALUES, AND CORE COMPETENCIES

Vision: To be the world leader in developing and delivering important cost-effective therapeutics based on advances in cellular and molecular biology.

Values:

Core Competencies:

- World's largest biotechnology firm
- Stock performance: 101 percent increase in 1995!
- Successful commercialization of products

YOUR PRODUCT OR SERVICE

Take a moment to think of what you could offer Amgen. Is there a fit between your product or service and Amgen's vision? Amgen's CEO and COO state that the company's transition from a two-product company to a many-product company is a major challenge. Would your product or service support this quest? Can you assist them in leveraging their core competencies?

TRENDMASTER TIPS AND PROVOCATIVE IDEAS

Review the information on the opposite page on the issues, trends, and developments affecting Amgen.

It is easy to feel intimidated reading Amgen's annual report. It is full of scientific terminology and medical jargon. I barely passed college biology, so I understand how you might feel. Stick with it, though, and you will find plenty to relate to. The objectives and issues given above are fundamental business areas where you can be of assistance. Additionally, when you are working with a health care company, you will want to consult the sample issues found in Chapter 7.

Take note of the fact that no values are listed for Amgen. Does that mean they don't have any? No specific references that could be interpreted as values were found in Amgen's annual report, but Hoover's company profile indicates that they have gone from operating at the brink of bankruptcy in 1983 to the world's largest biotechnology firm today. That is incredible. I know they are proud, and as a result I feel confident that they place a high value on entrepreneurial skills, perseverance, and resiliency. I would be sure to connect with the emotional power of these values.

Sometimes what is missing is as informative as what is visible. There was no reference to technology in Amgen's information. This could be a tremendous opportunity for a salesperson; for ex-

Expanding existing research collaborations and developing new ones
Licenses products and technologies from other companies
Intense competition
Tight expense control
Formal product portfolio review process
Acquisition of Synergen
Increased scrutiny in use of pharmaceuticals by health care providers

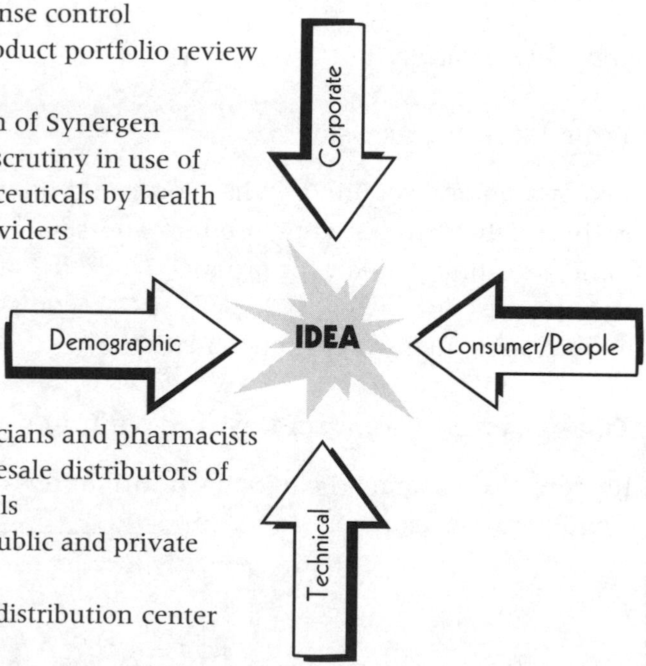

Markets to physicians and pharmacists
Uses major wholesale distributors of pharmaceuticals
Reimbursed by public and private payers
New West Coast distribution center

ample, what potential benefits do you notice in the diagram above for telecommunications services, such as use of the Internet for communication between scientists worldwide?

The Process

Now it's your turn. Complete the blanks in the following box and note the issues and trends that might affect your customer. Completing this exercise will help you assemble information that will lead to specific and valuable ideas of benefit to your customer.

Vision, Values and Core Competencies

Vision:

Values:

Core Competencies:

Your Product or Service

Take a moment to think of what you could offer __________. Is there a fit between your product and service and the customer's vision? Would your product or service support the customer's quest for ______________? Can you assist customers in leveraging their core competencies?

Trendmaster Tips and Provocative Ideas

Review the diagram below for information on the issues, trends, and developments affecting ____________________.

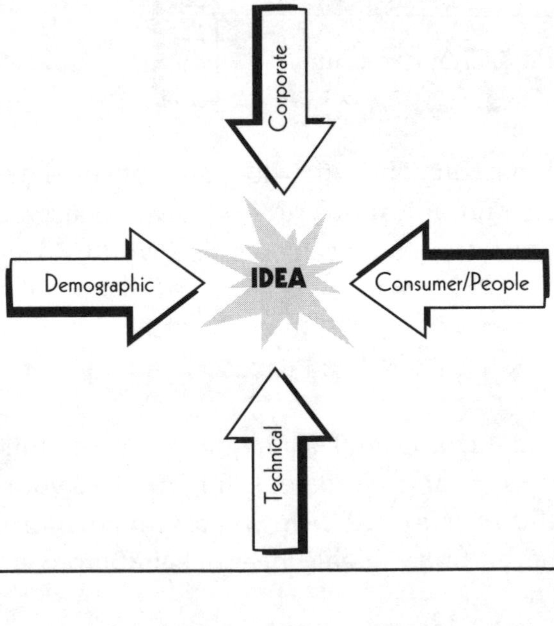

Corporate

Demographic

IDEA

Consumer/People

Technical

The "Killer Application"

Unique ideas and counterintuitive strategies have changed entire industries or even generations. The PC revolution is a classic. In 1980 few individuals felt the need for a personal computer. By 1990 many did. At what moment did the startling paradigm shift occur that changed the minds of an entire generation? Most experts agree it was exposure to Lotus 1-2-3 that caused this mental transformation. When a person changed one number on a spreadsheet and saw every affected number on the page change automatically, the result was "the Aha! heard around the world."

In high technology this is called the "killer application." It doesn't matter how many things a product can do, it becomes essential to most people only when a killer application is discovered—some capability or feature that is so valuable everyone believes he simply must have one as a result. Geoffrey Moore says a new product must "show that the new technology enables some strategic leap forward, something never before possible, which has an intrinsic value and appeal. This benefit is typically symbolized by a single, compelling application, the one thing that best captures the power and value of the new product."

The killer application exists for every industry, high or low tech. Look through your local newspaper tonight, for example, and notice the number of advertisements for luggage. In the *Los Angeles Times* I counted seven on a weekday and thirteen in a Sunday paper.

Several years ago, luggage was a stagnant industry. Most families bought luggage once, maybe twice, in a lifetime. Unless their luggage was worn out and they were about to embark on a vacation, buying new luggage was the furthest thing from their minds. The industry was plugging along at a low single-digit growth rate.

Then came roll-aboard luggage, the killer application. How many times did you notice other people coolly and calmly rolling their luggage behind them while you sweated and shifted the weight that was breaking your arm or numbing your shoulder before you invested in new luggage? Industry growth tripled overnight. Last year Americans spent $256.5 million on vertical carry-on flight bags, according to the Luggage and Leather Goods Manufacturers of America.

No industry is so boring, stable, mature, or secure that it cannot benefit from a killer application: an application that everyone must have, an application that brings the industry or product to the forefront of the minds of consumers, an application that doubles or triples or quadruples existing sales.

Every trend or demographic movement brings new opportunities for killer applications. In the late 1980s, affluent professionals who had delayed parenthood to focus on career began having children. The luxury minivan became a top seller. The girdle industry had been absolutely dead for the past thirty years. Suddenly, baby boomers started turning forty and fifty. The industry was reborn under the name of "shapers."

What if you, a salesperson, were the one to suggest a new idea with killer application potential to your customer or prospect? What if you helped your customer see an opportunity previously missed? Wouldn't you, in effect, be contributing to your customer's agenda and establishing the criteria? Isn't it likely you would be invited to stick around and develop the idea to fruition? To quote a marketing colloquialism, "If you are there at the conception, you are probably the father."

Form a "killer application" group. Choose four people from different industries and focus on one industry a month. Brainstorm as a group on every conceivable idea or invention that could revolutionize that industry. You will be the beneficiary of many valuable ideas.

The Quest

Imagine yourself generating such a hot idea that you would ask the person you meet with to sign a non-disclosure statement before you share it with him or her. Now that you have packaged the information, the challenge begins. Your quest is to discover patterns, originate ideas, and design solutions that are new and original.

Brilliant ideas and comprehensive solutions are holistic. They incorporate left brain logic and right brain creativity. In an elegant manner that neither omits critical information nor adds unnecessary clutter, the perfect idea or solution is simple and yet profound.

Tom Peters says he learns more about business from reading Franz Kafka than he does from reading a dozen business books. Mike Slade, CEO of Starwave, keeps two magazines on the coffee table in his office—*Nation's Business* and *MAD*. In my keynote speeches I often hold up *The Wall Street Journal* and *Fast Company* magazine, my own favorites, to illustrate that Visionary Selling encompasses both the pertinent and the provocative. Imagine my reaction when I read the following letter from Susan C. White, vice president of human resources for Simon & Schuster, in *Fast Company:* "Two weeks ago, I addressed a group of young people at my company. I held up two publications, *The Wall Street Journal* and *Fast Company,* and encouraged them to read both. I told them they'd find *The Journal* a bit boring but full of valuable business news. As for *Fast Company,* well, if they want to learn how to do business in the twenty-first century, they'd have to devour every page."

An article in *Fast Company,* "How Companies Have Sex" (a provocative title!) profiles Eric Schmidt, Sun Microsystems' chief technology officer. Eric's job is to spawn and nurture new businesses, which he does by creating a union of the fertile ideas of rebels and visionaries and the organizational DNA of Sun.

This is the quest of Visionary Selling: to find convergence between the pertinent and the provocative and then combine fertile ideas with the organizational DNA of your prospect or customer. Incorporate all relevant facts and then add a touch of magic. Craft a brilliant solution and then add a dose of soul. Make your prospect or customer say *Wow!*

A recent J. P. Morgan advertisement in *The Wall Street Journal* quoted Albert Szent-Gyorgyi, a biologist who received the Nobel Prize in 1937 for discovering vitamin C. I believe his statement summarizes the quest of Visionary Selling: "Research is to see what everybody else has seen, and to think what nobody else has thought."

Isn't This Risky?

Yes! The last step to success frequently requires a daring, intuitive leap. Once you feel a nibble, you have to hook the fish. Many people get a hunch, interpret it as a hunger pain, and go to lunch, instantly forgetting about it. Trust yourself. Trust your instincts.

Sure, it's a risk. But by taking the risk of being controversial and substantially more unorthodox, you can assist your customers as they define and integrate new paradigms. You can help them look beyond what is today and see what might be tomorrow. You can assist them as they imagine the future—and be around with them to enjoy it!

Visionary Selling Applied to a Hypothetical Case Study: StarSearch

The future is yours. You embark on a mission to boldly go where no one has gone before. The greatest group of engineers in the galaxy, working at warp speed, have created an awesome product that will transform personal lives and expand business productivity throughout the twenty-first century. The product is an intergalactic communicator called StarSearch, which allows communication between any two points in the galaxy. Your company has been selected as the sole distributor in quadrant one (aka Earth).

You have selected your first prospect, a humongous multigalactic pharmaceutical firm known for expanding the boundaries of business success by capitalizing on emerging communication technology. However, recent articles in the *Galaxy Journal* have mentioned that Gamma Pharmaceuticals is facing competitive pressure from companies that are duplicating their successful formula.

You have investigated Gamma and feel that the person who would be most interested in StarSearch is the chief information officer, Kathryn Klout. Kathryn is very visible in the business community and speaks frequently on "Revitalizing the Corporation Through Utilization of Enabling Technologies."

What are Gamma's Vision, Values, and Core Competencies?

After reviewing the company online and reading their annual report, you determine the following:

Vision: Gamma Pharmaceuticals is a world-class pharmaceutical company providing the industry's broadest range of pharmaceutical products supported by outstanding consumer education.

Values:

- Industry leader
- Education of consumer on value and application of pharmaceuticals
- Leading edge of information technology

Core Competencies:

- Research and development
- Respected by scientific community for ethics, standards, and quality
- Consumer communication

WHAT ISSUES ARE FACING THE PHARMACEUTICAL INDUSTRY?

From reading the trade press you have identified the following major issues:

- Branded drugs are under pricing pressure from generics.
- Insurance companies are refusing payment for "unproven" treatments.
- A significant aging trend appears in demographics.

EXPLORE TRENDS FOR GAMMA PHARMACEUTICALS

What is the trend?

The aging population is retiring to other planets and is difficult to reach with existing communication technology. This population is distrustful of business and business communications due to a medical industry scandal in the late twentieth century.

How will the trend manifest itself in my industry?

A significant percentage of the population is resistant to additional technology but is fascinated with the twentieth century and wants to return to "simpler times."

What are the implications of this trend for my industry? For my customers and prospects? For manufacturing, finance, sales and marketing, human resources?

Galactic markets
Challenges of intergalactic communication with customers
Lack of intergalactic information control

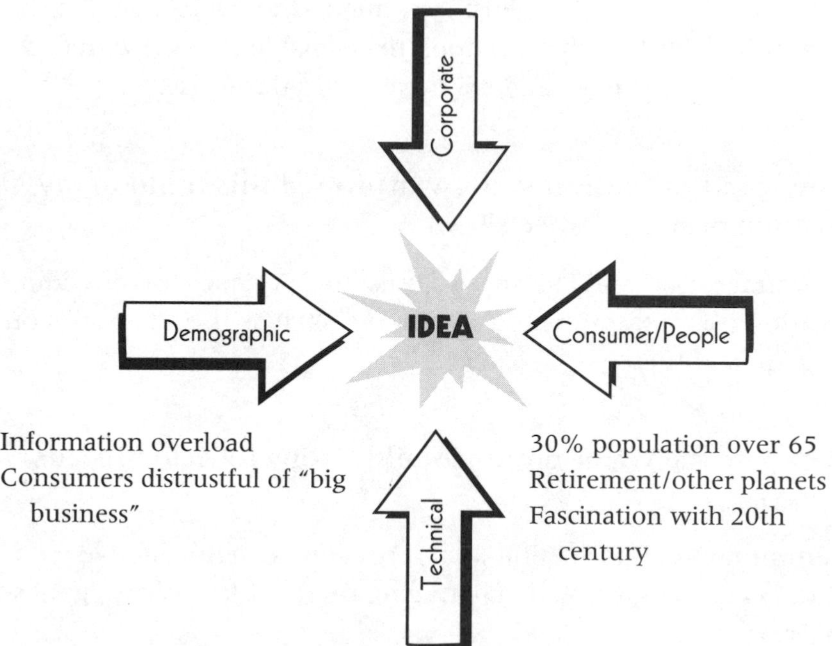

Consumers using "intelligent agents" to screen advertisements
New antiaging drugs

The trend creates an obstacle and an opportunity for your industry. Obstacle: A large portion of the population has moved to other planets to escape information overload and is overwhelmed by technology and distrustful of information received from businesses. Opportunity: The trend creates need for your product, since your customers and prospects *must* find effective ways of communicating with their customers.

How can I integrate information on this trend into my sales strategy?

Since consumers are clearly overwhelmed with advertising messages and distrustful of business, meet the issue head-on by presenting StarSearch as a tool that enables them to receive information they need and eliminate everything else.

How can I provide advance warning of this trend to my customers and prospects?

Encourage Gamma Pharmaceuticals to specialize in providing customers with information *they* value, such as the latest facts on health and fitness.

What are the major professional lessons reflected in this trend?

Communicate information that provides a demonstrable benefit to consumers instead of barraging them with advertising messages.

How is this trend likely to evolve in the coming years?

Consumers will block all advertising messages. They will be located throughout the universe, and business communication will be seriously challenged.

WHAT IS THE BEST WAY TO GAMMA PHARMACEUTICALS' CIO KATHRYN KLOUT?

You decide to capitalize on the opportunity of listening to Kathryn Klout speak and are rewarded with the following information drawn from her presentation:

1. Klout says, "We are getting to the point where our main business is providing information faster than our competitors."
2. One of Klout's hot buttons is the controversy between resistance to inter-galactic information censorship and the increase of incomplete, inaccurate, and even libelous information circulated on the Intergalactic Net.
3. There is a current media report regarding potential liability issues concerning one of Gamma Pharmaceuticals' key drugs, and Klout insinuates that it is untrue.
4. Klout relies heavily on E-mail for communication and to keep abreast of issues.

Thirty Ideas

1. People are living longer, but are they living better?
2. Isolation can lead to stress and depression.
3. There is a need for information on health, nutrition, and specific health issues.
4. Gamma needs a new profit center to replace expiring drug patents.
5. Gamma needs to get consumer trial data back to insurance companies faster to speed the approval process and claim reimbursement.
6. StarSearch could be programmed to beep trial participants several times daily to remind them to enter data.
7. People always want current information on new research/products if it is of benefit to them.
8. Intelligent agents could be programmed to personalize information and services.
9. StarSearch could use different codes for each family member.
10. Gamma could offer "frequent flyer" miles for accessing

information, participating in consumer trials, or buying products.

11. The intelligent agents could become more and more effective by asking consumers to rate articles after reading them.
12. A free StarSearch could be provided to customers with a specific illness and conditions that Gamma is researching, such as osteoporosis.
13. Customers could be provided free communication time to family and friends for frequent flyer miles.
14. Gamma could provide an option where their frequent flyer miles were donated to charities needing the service, such as nursing homes or foster homes.
15. All StarSearch communicators would provide an emergency life link feature.
16. A "Return to Simpler Times" advertising theme, similar to "Reach Out and Touch Someone," could be used to kick off the campaign.
17. Gamma would gain a competitive advantage by offering this additional service, thereby creating brand loyalty and luring consumers from generics.
18. Consumers could be prescreened for condition and risk factors.
19. StarSearch would "counsel and coddle" customers.
20. Two plans could be offered: For those over sixty-five, the primary benefit is staying in touch and receiving vital information; for those under sixty-five, the primary benefit is receiving health/fitness/lifestyle information.
21. The intelligent agent could visit Web sites, medical journals, and databases to customize a medical journal based on each patient's specific need for information on research and new treatments.
22. StarSearch could record information useful for prescreening and early diagnosis.

23. Customers could be paid to read advertisements or be offered discounts or frequent flyer miles.
24. StarSearch will be programmed with customers' prescribed medicines, to alert them to any side effects from adding another medicine.
25. Customers could receive updated risk factors on demand.
26. Customers could receive advance information on new developments.
27. Customers could receive free lifetime service after a certain number of years.
28. StarSearch could be programmed to remind them of checkups.
29. StarSearch would automatically file insurance claims.
30. StarSearch could provide daily hometown updates, including obituaries.

Pertinent and Provocative Story

Pertinent: Gamma Pharmaceuticals is facing erosion of its customer base from two factors: an inability to communicate product information to its primary market and competitive threats from less expensive generic drugs.

Gamma is also struggling to maintain a core competency/market advantage as a consumer education provider, since a large percentage of its market is out of reach of its communication channel or is resistant to receiving the information. Gamma is facing loss of revenue due to expiring patents on several key drugs. This could impact their investment in research and development, and diminish one of their core competencies.

Provocative: Gamma Pharmaceuticals can regain market leadership and create a new profit center. StarSearch will be positioned as a valuable technology that enables people to return to simpler times when they were geographically close to family and friends. An advertising campaign will present the question: You are living longer, but are you living better? The campaign will present three vital aspects of a long and healthy life: lifestyle, medical care (including emergency access), and information.

For participating customers, StarSearch will provide:

- Free life link service for emergency access to doctors and information.
- Personalized health and medical information, compiled in response to individual interests, health risk factors, medical conditions, nutrition, and exercise preferences. This information will become more and more specific to the individual, since an intelligent agent will respond to each one's rating of information.
- Encryption technology will neutralize privacy issues, and each family member will have a separate code.
- Hometown news.

CHAPTER 9
Present

Stop for a moment and think about how you usually present your product or service. Do you proceed through a specific format? Is the focus on demonstrating your product or describing your service? Do you place major emphasis on connecting benefits to needs or communicating a value proposition to close the sale?

With Visionary Selling you will acquire a whole new approach to one specific aspect of the sales process: presenting to executives. You will replace your standard process with a dynamic dialogue similar to brainstorming. You will not be describing or demonstrating your product or service at all. Perhaps the most shocking aspect for many of you: You will not be attempting to close the sale in this presentation.

Why? Let's take a look at who these people are.

The Visionary Perspective

In *Crossing the Chasm,* Geoffrey A. Moore profiles "early adopters" of new technology as "the visionaries . . . that rare breed of people who have the insight to match an emerging technology to a strategic opportunity, the temperament to translate that insight into a high-visibility, high-risk project, and the charisma to get the rest of their organization to buy into that project."

Specific components of this definition are associated with many top executives. To sell to a visionary you must integrate three key elements of Moore's definition into your sales presentation: Insight, translation, and charisma.

Perhaps most essential to our understanding of these powerful individuals and to our ability to create an alliance with them are the following insights from Moore's book: Visionaries are not looking for improvement; they are seeking a strategic breakthrough with an order of magnitude return. Moore states, *"Understand their dream, and you will understand how to market to them."*

For example, Paul Allen was cofounder of Microsoft and is a current investor in myriad new ventures that he hopes will create a technorevolution. According to an article in the *Los Angeles Times,* any company or inventor who can aid that quest has Allen's immediate attention.

How can you capture attention and then establish a productive business relationship with a visionary individual? You must understand that visionaries are big thinkers with big ideas and big dreams. Their frame of reference is seven to ten or more years in the future. They are willing to accept a high level of risk for the potential return of seeing their dream or vision materialize. It is your job to discover (insight) and then demonstrate the link (translation) between their dream and your product or service.

Visionaries don't buy, they envision, paint a picture. Your picture may create a picture in their minds. And that is the whole idea.

Return on Investment of Time

Top executives are very focused. That is why and how they ascended to the top. They evaluate opportunities and make decisions in terms of return on investment, and that includes every single minute of their time. The "C" level has advanced by earning the greatest possible return on every resource, and one of the greatest resources we possess is our time. Top executives expect dividends for every second they invest.

This intense focus changes the rules of business associations. The "C" level will measure its investment of time by the results achieved. It is up to you to ensure that these executives are astounded and not disappointed by the results of a meeting with you.

When meeting with the "C" level, do not waste time on small talk. Do not invest valuable moments attempting to establish rapport. Establishing rapport is absolutely unnecessary. Your clear and concise communication of a potentially valuable idea will establish all the rapport needed, and if you are unable to do that, rapport will be of no use to you. These executives are not looking for friends. They are not looking for an ongoing business relationship. They are looking for compelling new ideas and approaches, or people who can challenge their paradigms and help them formulate new ideas and approaches. Period.

Eliminate chitchat! Get right to the point. Unless you have something powerful to say, listen.

Preparation is Vital

This leads to the next point. Top executives expect you to be prepared. You have about thirty seconds to attract or repel them. If you repel them, it is unlikely you will get a second opportunity. And you will know right away if this happens. They might pounce and begin interrogating you, or they might simply drift off, break eye contact, and begin shuffling papers or looking around. If they finish listening before you finish speaking, you've blown it.

You will also know if you have hooked them. When this happens, they will take your idea and run with it. It is a fabulous thing to observe. Sometimes they begin talking to themselves, exploring the idea and its potential. It is as if you are no longer in the room. Sometimes they jump in and begin selling your idea back to you, perhaps in a totally unrecognizable form.

When this happens, do you interrupt their reverie and remind them you are still there? Do you correct them if they have changed your idea into one of their own? Of course not! This is exactly what you are shooting for. It has been said that every person who buys does so by changing your idea into their idea. Nowhere is this statement more true than at the "C" level. They do not buy; they envision. And if what they envision includes you, you have scored. They will work out the details. Their people will call your people.

Portray Confidence and Courage

If you are feeling anxious right now, I understand. Just the thought of meeting with a CEO or CFO can cause fear to well up in your chest and dance a rumba in your throat. A lot of effort will be required just to get you there. The last thing you want to do is alienate this person you have worked so hard to meet. Right?

Visionary Selling requires information, intelligence, insight, but most of all *courage*. It requires courage to be open to new thoughts. It requires courage to integrate these ideas into customer opportunities. It especially requires courage to present these innovative ideas to top executives.

The thought of approaching a top-level executive with an innovative idea may give you butterflies. You might feel that an appointment with a CEO is the time when you want most to be on solid ground, feeling comfortable and confident, with a broad base of information and substantiated facts to back up every idea you present.

Would it increase your openness to this approach if I told you that Steven Spielberg confided in an interview that he begins each movie wondering if he can pull it off or if this time he is in over his head? He claims he arrives at the movie studio each morning with butterflies in his stomach. The creative geniuses we admire most have learned to live with butterflies, since the ambiguity and uncertainty that nourish butterflies are vital components of the creative process.

Despite your butterflies, you must exude an aura of confidence and charisma when meeting with top executives. Is this how most people respond? Hardly! Many people instantly lose their natural charm when in the presence of someone who is very important. To cover their anxiety, some become defensive and arrogant. They act as if the interaction is a contest. Swaggering and posturing will get you nowhere. People who act like that are fired.

On the other hand, some individuals who are successful, articulate, and confident are transformed into stammering wimps when they come face-to-face with a person who has been featured in newspaper articles or television interviews.

The "C" level has no time for wimps. The executives on this level place maximum value on courage, power, and self-assurance. Having achieved success by confidently and forcefully communicating their ideas, they respect others who do the same. Top executives believe in themselves and in their ability to understand things others cannot, so they live by their own counsel and ignore the naysayers. They illustrate the adage "The moon could not go on shining if it paid attention to little dogs barking at it."

You must have the courage to stand toe-to-toe with them and communicate your ideas. By portraying the same confidence in your ideas and in your ability to understand things others cannot, you place yourself in their league. Anyone who becomes intimidated is not in their league. Anyone who lacks courage and commitment to their ideas is not in their league. Anyone who could be discouraged or demotivated by rejection is not in their league. They are looking for people who are bold in their ideas and firm in their convictions.

Robert J. Kriegel claims in his book *If It Ain't Broke . . . BREAK IT!* that playing it safe is dangerous. He stresses the fact that "peak performers are bold and daring; they don't play it safe, they don't play not to lose."

What does playing "not to lose" mean? If you are careful and cautious in your communication with the "C" level, you are playing not to lose. But lose you will, because you have wasted their time, a precious resource. Only by playing to win, taking chances, and going for it do you gain the opportunity to connect. Trust your intuition and instincts. The top executives may or may not respond favorably to what you are communicating this time, but they will perceive you as a bold idea person who has the confidence to communicate innovative, controversial ideas. And that quality is gold to them.

Combine a demeanor of assurance and confidence with your sincere feelings of admiration and respect. Respond like the woman in the joke who was told by a CEO that he couldn't see her and she should come back in ten years. "Morning or afternoon?" she asked. Do you think the CEO was convinced of her commitment to working with him and her earnest dedication to establishing a relationship?

When I was writing *Secrets of Peak Performers,* I felt honored to be with people who had achieved high levels of success and had such valuable knowledge to impart. I was totally alert and attentive, more alert and attentive than I have ever been in my life. And they were honored by my obvious respect for them and for what they could teach me.

Remember Leo Rivera from Chapter 2 who targeted Eastman Kodak and met with the CEO? After attending a "step-up" sales training class that promoted selling higher in the corporation, she was excited to get started. When some of her peers said they were nervous at the thought, Leo said, "You've got to be kidding. What could be more of a thrill than to touch the hand of someone like George Fisher?"

I believe the best mental model is "a young version of themselves." It seems to be a fundamental human response to support and assist others after you attain a high level of personal success and influence. Most individuals at the "C" level advanced by being mentored. Now that they have "arrived," they are mentoring others. These activities are natural and rewarding to them.

You will find that most regard salespeople with respect. They admire the combination of motivation, confidence, and entrepreneurial skills a salesperson must have to compete in the marketplace. Either they are great salespeople themselves, or their past and future success depends on great salespeople. A great salesperson will identify with your talent, but one who is not will admire and appreciate you (and perhaps instruct someone to try to hire you).

Design Insightful, Specific Questions

Before your appointment or call to the "C" level, craft three to five specific, insightful questions. The best questions combine an obvious knowledge of the company and industry, a touch of controversy or challenge, and a request for information the executives like to talk about. I call these "key" questions because they open a door by getting the customer to open up and reveal what was hidden before. Whenever you ask a question that leads to several moments of valuable information being shared, make a note that that is a potential "key" question and use it again. Spend more time crafting your questions than you do devising your answers.

Sample Questions to Ask the "C" Level

What is the biggest threat facing your industry?

What is the biggest opportunity for your industry in the next decade?

Where is the stock market value migrating to in your industry? (that is, Sears to Wal-Mart, private physicians to HMOs, mainframes to PCs to Internet access devices)?

What is the most exciting future market for your company?

What are your biggest customers asking for?

What would it take to provide that?

Do you see more opportunity in expanding current products/ services or venturing into new markets?

Is your company focusing on increasing revenues or market share?

A word of caution: Keep your questions free of corporate buzzwords. A glossary of important financial and business terms is included in Appendix II. I suggest you become familiar with them so that you understand what is said and know where it is leading. If a term is used by an executive that you don't understand, ask what it means. Asking for clarification is a lot more intelligent than assuming you know what the word means and possibly responding inappropriately. Don't use any term until your customer does; if you start tossing around the latest lingo, you will probably look as ridiculous as the memorandum below.

Memo to Associates:

In benchmarking our company's performance against a peer group since our recent reengineering, we realize that further rightsizing is in order to achieve the efficiencies needed to return to our core competencies. To ensure that this continues to be a high-performance workplace, we will begin outsourcing our human resources functions and convert other departments into cross-functional teams. A paradigm shift is necessary if we are to remain a learning organization in an era of discontinuous change. Our vision is that you empowered intrapreneurs, along with our fast-growing contingent workforce, will think out of the box as we implement total quality processes. Our change management expert will contact you to explain our utilization of 360-degree feedback as part of our transformation to a pay-for-performance model.

Yours in excellence,
Learning Officer I. M. Master

A valuable key question, if the company is familiar with stretch goals, might be: "What are your company's stretch goals?" If the company is not familiar with stretch goals, the question could create feelings of confusion, ignorance, or boredom. The last thing you want to do is imply that you know more about management theory or leadership skills than your customer does.

Do Some Listening Before You Do Any Talking

Once you have obtained an appointment with the "C" level, the most important skill is *listening!* You demonstrate a genuine dedication to establishing an alliance with your prospect when you ask insightful, intelligent questions with a high degree of specificity and then *listen.*

Recently I attended an appointment with Joanne Murachver from Symantec, one of the world's leading software companies. Shortly after introductions, the prospect began talking about issues and objectives. "We've been going through so much change around here," he said.

If this had been my appointment, I would have seized the opportunity to commiserate by saying, "Oh, I know. Aren't the nineties wild? All my clients are going through so much change."

Joanne resisted this pitfall. "Why is that?" she asked, and she was rewarded with ten minutes of specific, valuable information.

My instinctive response, to interrupt and agree, would have been totally ineffective. "Why is that?" is brilliant. After all, there are differences between the change that follows downsizing and the change that accompanies growth. There are differences between cost cutting due to decreased revenues and cost cutting to fuel corporate expansion. If you don't ask, you won't know.

When I began my career in sales, I knew absolutely nothing about how to sell. I knew slightly more than nothing about the technical and fast-moving field of telephony that I had entered. I knew a little about the company, MCI, that I worked for. Despite this lack of knowledge and my feelings of inadequacy, my sales numbers were phenomenal!

Months later I knew an enormous amount. I had read every book on the market on selling skills. I knew enough about telephony to be dangerous. I had memorized the story of David and Goliath—MCI versus AT&T—and could tell it like a grand champion of the toastmasters tall tales event. And my numbers had sunk through the ground.

Why? People would rather talk than listen. People buy more when they're talking than when they're listening. People are most happy talking about themselves and are least happy listening to someone else talk about themselves.

For salespeople, this can be a challenge. Many of us entered the profession of sales because we love to communicate, to share ideas and solutions and to articulate information that we feel is important or valuable. Most salespeople would fit right into a T-shirt I saw in a beachfront souvenir shop: HELP! I'M TALKING AND I CAN'T SHUT UP!

Salespeople are adept at expressing ideas, opinions, and emotions. However, we often meet with people who are more introverted and less open in their communication than we are. Since they have to warm up their communication engines, allow them time to idle for a few moments. You will be surprised at how much they have to say once they get going. Do not interrupt them once they've gotten started. They are not nearly as quick to resume communicating as we are, and an interruption can stop the flow permanently.

On your next appointment, try this experiment: Every time you feel the urge to communicate a point, remain silent and see what happens next. *Whatever you hear next is information you would not have received if you were talking.*

While they are talking, you listen intently. Top executives have strong opinions and brilliant ideas. There is no one they find more fascinating than themselves. Many visionary individuals develop their ideas and insights through the dialogue process. A conversation with a stimulating individual who listens with rapt attention may lead them to a discovery about their dream or vision. If you are the stimulus that allows them to see something in a new way or to encounter a new thought, they will love you for it.

Your high-level dialoguing with a top executive will also produce ideas of value to you and your company. Many companies, including my own, have identified future product and market opportunities through feedback gained in the sales process. Several years ago I met with the CEO of Club Sportswear. Tom Knapp and I were discussing ideas for their national sales meeting. "We need a high-energy meeting that improves morale," Tom said, "and it has to be fun." "How about games?" I responded. Tom jumped at the idea, which resulted in a very successful sales meeting that achieved his objectives and led to development of the Klue Sales Training Game for me.

Record the conversation on a microcassette if permitted. That way you can pay rapt attention as the executives speak, without the distraction of note-taking. All the fabulous ideas that emerge from your meeting will be captured for you to work with.

Focus on their words and the meaning behind their words. Record specific phrases, framed in quotation marks or in a special color ink (green makes sense) so you will remember exactly what was said. Their words are *magic.*

An article about one of my top prospects appeared in an obscure magazine The article quoted the vice president of sales and mentioned that the beauty of the company was that it was different and unique. I left a message on voice mail for the VP, saying that "the beauty of my program is that it is different and unique, and that is what your company is all about." By the end of the day I received a call from one of his assistants who used my words: "The beauty of your program is that it is different and unique, and that is what our company is all about." By the end of the month I was working with him.

What happens when an executive hears his words repeated? If he doesn't recognize the words as his own, he will feel a sense of alliance and connectedness. If he does, he will be flattered that you took the time to research his philosophies and opinions. Your investment of time and energy to discover who the executives on the "C" level are and what they think will be viewed as indicative of your commitment to your customers. Either way, you win.

One of the biggest areas of apprehension for salespeople as they begin targeting executives is that they won't understand what they are saying. This concern is valid, so I won't ignore or sugarcoat it. Although you will control the situation as much as possible with thorough preparation, top executives move in a world that is different from yours and are familiar with concepts and ideas that may sound like a foreign language to you. You don't want to look like an idiot. How do you communicate with people whose knowledge and ideas may be beyond your scope?

Listen to them and write everything down! Their interest is in communicating information to you that may lead to a successful, strategic outcome for them. They did not meet with you to explore your intelligence or expertise; they met with you to achieve results. You will not impress them with your clever verbal repartee; you will impress them with your commitment to do whatever it takes to give them what they want. This often means collecting information and acting as a conduit within your company to find the right people to take the next step.

Mike Newman of 3M met with a key executive at Motorola who claimed that 3M was developing a technology that could answer a strategic need of Motorola's. Mike didn't have a clue what the executive was talking about. Since he said it over and over again, Mike knew it was important. He began writing everything down (a tape recorder would have been very handy here.) He spent weeks at 3M attempting to uncover the information and enlisted a scientist for the return appointment. The end result was a greater understanding of the capabilities of each company, greater respect between the two, and discovery of strategic opportunities with significant potential.

Record every meeting with an executive on a microcassette if he or she permits.

Follow Their Lead

Shortly after I started my own business, at a time when I needed my first "break," I scheduled an appointment with the executive vice president of a huge wholesale pharmaceutical drug distributor by communicating a fairly wild idea over the phone. When I entered his office, he jumped up, grabbed my arm, and asked if we could talk outside while he had a cigarette. We sat at a table on the patio, and I began my presentation. After less than one minute, he grabbed the portfolio I was using for reference and began to rustle through it. Within three minutes he had thrown my carefully prepared proposal onto the table and was pitching me with an idea. He had always wanted to add a motivational vignette to the end of the company's video newsletter that was distributed monthly to the field sales force. Would I be interested in creating and presenting these vignettes, to be videotaped in their production studio?

During that appointment, which lasted about five minutes, I never said more than a few hundred words. I walked out of the building with my head spinning and my future (or at least the next three months) secure. If a prospect seizes your idea and runs with it, follow his or her lead. If the prospect doesn't respond to your idea within five minutes, you may be on the wrong track. Back off and resume asking questions.

You may be wondering about the wild idea that captured the executive vice president's attention. In an attempt to increase the use of creativity, visualization, and outside-the-box thinking in sales proposals and presentations, I was using a startling mind-opening exercise called warm forming, where participants would actually bend metal spoons using the power of mental concentration. After a period of intense focus, the hard metal spoon would become warm and pliable enough to be bent and twisted. I never did this exercise or this program for the company, but the idea was provocative enough to get me in the door. Once there, my contact bought my idea by turning it into one of his own—to add a taped vignette featuring new sales ideas and approaches to an existing format.

Communicate Concisely

Practice your ability to communicate creative ideas in sound bites. As a result of total media immersion, most of us are programmed to respond to thirty-second messages. When dealing with busy executives, this communication skill is vital for maximum impact. Practice over and over how you will communicate your idea in the most compelling style possible in thirty seconds or less.

One of the best methods of doing this is by using metaphor or analogy. Reflect on your idea until it is clear in your mind. Now ask yourself, "What is it like?" Search for metaphors that capture the essence of your idea and that will help others to understand what you mean.

Prepare a Meeting Agenda

If you are familiar with the company, its goals and objectives, and the vision of the leader, you may want to prepare an agenda for the meeting. Fax this agenda to the company in advance of the meeting. This will allow the executives an opportunity to amend it to fit their purposes. They are so focused on optimization of resources, including their time, that they require an agenda for just about any activity. Play the game by their rules, and you increase your chance of winning.

The agenda should encourage rather than stifle open-ended discussion of unresolved needs, market opportunities, potential alliances, and future direction.

Stop Talking Before They Stop Listening

Remember the value the top executives place on their time. Once you are seated with them and things are going well, you may forget the importance of brevity. Top executives often possess superior people skills and are adept at helping others feel comfortable and even fascinating. You may be lulled into a false sense of camaraderie.

Have you ever had an interesting but long-winded conversation with a colleague or a coworker? Even though you enjoyed the conversation at the time, the next time that person called, your first thought was to make an excuse to avoid another lengthy interaction. You simply did not have the time.

Guard against the tendency to feel that the meeting is going so well you should extend it. George Bennett, senior vice president of sales and marketing for ATC Communications, suggests ending the meeting before they do. This action will demonstrate your respect for their time. George also suggests you always finish with a hook that gives you a reason to come back. This leads to our next point.

Anchor the Value

In a typical sales presentation you would ask for the business. Remember, the "C" level does not buy; it envisions. In this appointment you will not be asking for the business. The moment you shift into a selling mode, you change the dynamic of the relationship. *Don't do it!*

This might be the hardest part for most salespeople to accept. They live to close the sale. Their sales manager demands it. How can I even suggest such a travesty?

If you have captured the executives' attention and struck a nerve, they will determine the next step. If you have not, the most important objective is that you leave the door open for a return engagement. Which of the two occurs is completely up to them. You are not in control of the situation; they are.

You do control your parting words, however. Think about it. The last minute is your final communication. That makes your parting words very important, since they determine the impression you leave. If you're like most people, though, you spend a lot more time thinking about your entrance than your exit. As a result, many presentations simply trickle to a close.

What are your objectives with this final communication if not to get the business? You are striving to create a state of mind—their state of mind about you and your value. You want them to feel that the time spent with you was a good investment. You cannot afford to leave this critical appraisal to chance. You must cement the value of your time with them in their mind right now so that when you call back in one month or one year, they will remember they associated a value to the time invested today.

Ask them. The "C" level appreciates direct communications and people who can make a point. Take the time to script two to three sentences. Focus on the connection you have formed either by understanding their vision or by offering industry foresight. Briefly explain that you invested a lot of thought and effort preparing for your meeting with them, and it is important for you to know if they felt the time they spent with you had value.

The response you receive determines the direction you will take in proceeding. If one of your ideas clicked or a positive synergy was established, you may ask for a referral if they have not already provided one. If they agree it was a good meeting with valuable input and information, ask if you may contact them again in the future or if there is anyone else in the company or among their network you should meet with. If they did not obtain any value from the meeting, ask them why and listen carefully to the response. This information is critical for future contact with this prospect and for your future development.

Write down what they say word for word. When you contact them again, you will use these words to remind them of the positive experience they had when meeting with you.

At the end of your appointments with executives, ask them whom they most admire. Then read a biography of the people mentioned. You will gain tremendous insight into their values and their nature.

Ten-Step Checklist for a "C" Level Appointment

Prepare, prepare, prepare.
Enter the room with the essential ingredient: self-confidence.
Display your honor and respect.
Ask pertinent, insightful questions and *listen.*
Trust your instincts.
Communicate concisely and courageously.
Present your most powerful idea.
If the prospects or customers don't run with it in five minutes or less, resume asking questions.
Script your close.
Play to win.

CHAPTER 10
New Value/New Enjoyment

The time has come to revolutionize the profession of sales. Every single aspect of business has undergone a radical metamorphosis in the last decade. Now it is our turn.

It is time for those of us who have received intense satisfaction and rich rewards from the profession of sales to collectively take our careers to the next tier, to steepen the curve, to expand the boundaries of sales, to revolutionize our profession by increasing the value we offer to our customers, and to renew our sense of fulfillment by catapulting to more challenging and exciting levels of creative problem solving and innovative thinking.

Want to enjoy the profession of sales more? Put more of yourself into it. Picture yourself as the highest-level professional you can imagine, one who understands business in general and your customers specifically—so well that you can ask thought-provoking questions, engage in stimulating discussions, and design visionary strategic collaborations.

Who Are You, Anyway?

After fifteen years of being a salesperson, managing salespeople, and working side by side with salespeople, this is what I know about you. You are boldly intelligent. Your curiosity is insatiable. You have a hunger for novelty and constantly seek new ways of looking at things and new methods of achieving results.

You are imaginative, innovative, and creative. You like to toy with ideas. You are fascinated by complex problems, intriguing challenges, and the most frustrating of brain teasers. (Who do you think bought all those Rubik's Cubes?) If I hand you a problem so puzzling and aggravating that it would drive many people over the edge, you will perk up and ponder the problem from all angles until you have the perfect solution (with a little sizzle thrown in for good measure).

You are also highly entrepreneurial. This is fortunate, since the sales profession requires that you reinvent your world daily. Anytime you doubt that you are really in business for yourself, let those numbers slide for three or four months and then measure your job security. It is entrepreneurial drive that enables salespeople to get up every single day and motivate themselves to create a job. When you are in sales, no one gives you a stack of work to do for the day. You create it. No one is waiting by the phone for you to call. You initiate it. You build your own job day by day. As they say, you make it happen.

Why Do Salespeople Fail?

With this exemplary combination of skills and abilities, why do salespeople fail? They get bored. They get into a rut. They begin to feel like a parrot, calling people over and over and saying the same thing day after day. For an intelligent, creative, entrepreneurial individual, this is a fate worse than death. Boredom is the ultimate torture, and routine is poison.

Why do salespeople fail? Because they do not perceive sales as a valued and valuable profession! It is true: Sales began as a sleazy profession. If you doubt this, imagine a snake oil salesperson hawking products from the side of a truck, making ludicrous promises, and beating it out of town just before the townspeople organized a lynching.

Just for fun, use the thesaurus feature on your word processor to locate synonyms for the word "sell." Here is what I found: exchange, barter, trade, bargain, retail, vend, peddle. Wait! It gets better: betray, deceive, violate, fail, disappoint.

If you have ever had mixed feelings about your chosen profession of sales, this may provide a clearer understanding of your conflict.

Not so long ago we considered superior sales performance the ability to persuade people to buy things they didn't want or need. Today we have moved beyond selling refrigerators to Eskimos. Salespeople today are intelligent and educated. They had a choice of many careers; they selected sales because they regard it as a worthy profession. They are selling with dignity by honoring their customers and prospects.

There is another reason why salespeople fail. They feel they have no control. They regard sales as a roller-coaster ride. Some sales fall into their lap unearned, while others that they have earned several times over fall through. It can be nerve-racking to base your livelihood on a career that sometimes defies comprehension or explanation. It gets tiresome calling the Psychic Friends Network to see if you will make quota.

For several years I have been surveying top salespeople asking, "How did you get into sales?" Most have responded with stories of an accidental career choice. When I ask why they stay, the real irony emerges. Top salespeople find the profession of sales so fascinating and so frustrating that they would be bored doing anything else. Why fascinating? Because top salespeople are exposed to an incredible range of people, ideas, and problems. Why frustrating? For the same reason and one more.

How many of you work for a company that supports and promotes a consultative selling style, with the focus on the customer's needs and objectives? And yet what does your manager say when you return from a sales appointment? "Did you get it? Did you get the order?" Sound familiar? As one of my customers says, "We are really into strategic selling here, but only for the first part of the quarter."

This creates an emotional catch-22 for salespeople. This is why you often feel anxious, conflicted, and drained. Countless books, audiocassettes, and training classes have conditioned you to focus on your customers and do what is right for them, rather than focusing on your own need for an order, commission, or quota. But it is not completely true, is it?

On an airplane recently I found myself staring at the screen for the in-flight phone, which was situated directly in front of me. It continuously flashed these words: "Got the sale? Call your boss. Didn't get it? Call your headhunter." Let's face it: The purpose of sales is to get the business. The purpose of a salesperson is to sell. To pretend otherwise is to create conflict and anxiety for individuals trying to reconcile two opposing messages.

The Quest for Meaningful Work

One of the dominant human trends of the 90s is the quest for meaning and purpose in one's work. Our parents were satisfied with a secure job and career advancement. We want more. We want our work to make a difference. We want to perform with passion. Is this asking too much of a career in sales? I don't think so. In *Business as a Calling: Work and the Examined Life* by Michael Novak, the author claims, "Business has the potential, at least, to serve as a 'calling'—a unique expression of aptitudes and aspirations that are larger than the sum of our daily duties."

The part of our work in sales that provides the greatest long-term meaning and fulfillment is the connection with people. To ease anxiety, to smooth out the rough spots, to provide a sense of trust and partnership in our clients is what many of us would define as our "calling." And yet our job description is to produce sales.

Write a vision or mission statement for your career. Ask yourself some hard-hitting questions: Where is there congruency? Where is there conflict?

The Paradox

A paradox emerges. The greatest passion and contribution for salespeople, who are always searching for deeper fulfillment in their careers, is developing rapport, building relationships, and resolving complex problems. Since corporations must increase quarterly earnings to meet analysts' expectations and retain market capitalization, however, salespeople are hammered by intense pressure to produce constantly increasing sales results by the end of the quarter. Can these two perspectives be reconciled? I believe so, and once again I assert that we need a new sales paradigm that acknowledges and confronts the realities of a sales career in the 1990s.

"Partnership selling" teaches you to put the customer's needs and objectives first. Your sales manager wants you to sell your product. How can you resolve these competing perspectives?

It is impossible to hold two contradictory thoughts in your mind at the same time. Try it. Think about good and evil simultaneously. Try golf and quota. You can't do it. You can alternate and even pulse quickly back and forth between the two, but you can focus on only one at a time.

Which is it? Your customer's perspective or yours? Somebody has to come first, and your customer can tell who it is!

We battle this challenge in sales every day. Let's stop fighting. Let's eliminate the mental stress of the conflict, and free all that wasted energy to focus on a method that will put our customers' needs for successful ideas and solutions and our need to sell products and services on an equal footing. Let's discover a sales approach that achieves both!

The Evolution of Marketable Skills

Much has been written recently about a workplace revolution that is replacing the world we know with a new world of work. In the old world, muscle power was in great demand, and wealth was created by producing or manufacturing commodities such as steel or cars or fuel. The new world of work is brainpower-driven. Wealth is increasingly created by producing ideas. "Intellectual capital" is the new source of competitive advantage. The personal and professional credentials required to thrive in an era of intellectual capital are critical thinking, problem solving, openness to novel ideas and new ways of doing things, and an ability to synthesize information into unique and useful products and services.

Major companies today have a Wall Street valuation that far exceeds their physical assets; for example, Microsoft has $7.2 billion in physical assets, but the value of its outstanding stock is $69.4 billion. How do you account for the additional $62.2 billion? Knowledge, talent, and brainpower.

If you are anything like most salespeople I've encountered, you are constantly coming up with unusual and original ideas. You love to think and invent. The entrepreneurial side of you has always secretly hoped that one of your red hot ideas would someday catapult you into the ranks of the rich and famous, so you can watch as *your* house is described in breathtaking detail on Robin Leach's *Lifestyles of the Rich and Famous:* "And here, beyond the sculpted gardens reminiscent of the Medici era in Renaissance Italy, are the tennis courts."

If you believe what I am saying in this book, you understand that your customers are requesting and demanding more of your creative brainpower than ever before. As we approach the third millennium, it appears that a well-tuned mind and mentally agile approach are considered by some companies to be requirements for employment!

Think of the questions you answered on your last job interview: Where do you see yourself in five years? What is your greatest strength? Describe a time you failed and what you learned from the experience. Microsoft has an unconventional approach to interviewing prospective candidates using brainteaser questions to identify the type of intelligence that thrives at Microsoft. Two samples:

1. You wake up one morning and there's been a power outage. You know you have twelve black socks and eight blue ones. How many socks do you need to pull out before you have a match?
2. Why are manhole covers round?

I often include these questions in my keynote presentation just to test my theory that salespeople are closet geniuses who love to ponder complex and puzzling riddles. Sure enough, at least a few people will come up afterward and provide answers. The amazing and exciting part is that the answers are never the same!

Creativity in Sales

I realize that you may feel uncomfortable with the idea of applying a creative approach to your work. You may feel that as a sales professional your company and your customers demand solutions that are logical, analytically sound, and technically feasible. Most of us are more comfortable approaching a business issue through a rational, linear process. However, according to Edgar de Bono, author of thirty-six books on creative thinking, approaching problems from several different angles simultaneously produces a breakthrough idea or solution. He calls this lateral thinking, which is multidimensional and incorporates a myriad of facts and ideas, as opposed to linear thinking, which proceeds in a straight line from A to B.

The capacity for making intuitive decisions is a basic ingredient of creativity. In *Crossing the Chasm,* Geoffrey Moore claims that informed intuition rather than analytical reason is the most trustworthy decision-making tool to use in high-risk, low-data decisions. He says, "Despite our culture's anxiety about relying on nonverbal processes, there are situations in which it is simply more effective to substitute right-brained tactics for left-brained ones. Ask any great athlete, or artist, or charismatic leader—ask any great decision maker. All of them describe a similar process, in which analytical and rational means are used extensively both in preparation for and in review of a central moment of performance. But in the moment itself, the actual decisions are made intuitively."

Business today is packed with high-risk, low-data decisions. As a result, informed intuition has become a powerful business tool.

Jamming: The Art and Discipline of Business Creativity by John Kao uses a jazz jam session as a metaphor for the creative process. Kao's definition of the creative process is summarized in the book's description of jam: "to take a theme, a question, a notion, a whim, an idea, pass it around, break it up, put it together, turn it over, run it backward, fly with it as far as possible, out of sight, never retreating . . . but yes, here it comes, homing in, changed, new, the essence, like nothing ever before."

Like any new process or skill, this one improves with practice. If you have always followed a formula in your sales activities, just thinking about stepping outside your current sales role is a good first step. If you have used creativity extensively to resolve customer issues and needs, it will be easier for you to begin thinking outside the box to provide ideas and resources to your customers. Either way, investing time and energy in developing the visionary in you can reap a huge payoff.

Salespeople as Master Idea Generators

The time is right for salespeople to step into a role that fits their personalities and skill sets perfectly: master idea generator. In the past five years the concepts of innovation, creativity, and outside-the-box thinking have stepped into the business spotlight as sound competitive strategies. Pick up any business book or magazine today, and you will discover a chapter or an article on business creativity, a phrase that would have been considered an oxymoron ten years ago.

In the January 1996 issue of *Management Review,* an article by Oren Harari claims, "In a brain-based economy, the winning organizations will be those that can generate the greatest number of interesting ideas, take rapid-fire action on them, and then disseminate immediate feedback to everyone so as to generate more ideas."

Harari goes on to instruct corporations to generate, consolidate, and use ideas from every possible source. He specifically names employees, customers, suppliers, partners, and outside experts. He does not name salespeople, unless we consider ourselves included in the generic category of suppliers. This concerns me. What better source than salespeople to supply insight and ideas?

Many of your customers are so busy and immersed in their businesses that they fail to see beyond the corporate lobby. They look to you to bring them news of the outside world. They may not have had time for several weeks to read anything other than office memos. Imagine the value you provide as you bring news of academic studies, marketing surveys, and demographic trends.

Establishing a Connection

Analyze your customers and prospects. Look closely at how they act, the words they say, and the meaning behind the words. Are they calm, secure, and contented? Or are they anxious, frustrated, and frightened? According to Warren Bennis, "Even the still-employed are in a chronic state of anxiety. A demoralizing sense of powerlessness is what many job holders are feeling. Nearly everyone worries about getting a pink slip."

And then there is technology. We face a daily media assault that seems calculated to make us feel guilty, inadequate, ignorant, or soon to be obsolete if we do not understand the latest technological trend and spend our evenings "surfin' the net." I have customers at the "C" level who do not have keyboarding skills. They do not know how to move a mouse. For them, the Internet is the Inter*not!* How secure do you think they are? And every reference to the "Age of the Net" brings their anxiety to the surface.

Customers are nervous and unsettled, unsure of where they want to go or how to get there. In his landmark book *The Courage to Create* (published in 1975 but compiled from writings of the 50s and 60s), Rollo May states,

> We are living at a time when one age is dying and the new age is not yet born. We cannot doubt this as we look about us to see the radical changes in sexual mores, in marriage styles, in family structures, in education, in religion, technology, and almost every other aspect of modern life. . . . A choice confronts us. Shall we, as we feel our foundations shaking, withdraw in anxiety and panic? If we do, we will have surrendered our chance to participate in the forming of the future."

Let's participate in the forming of the future. Let's determine how to sell in an era of intense and continuous change. Let's seize the opportunity created by the 3 R's of the 90s, with the top executive level more accessible to salespeople than ever before and more receptive to outside sources of information.

We have the formula to connect with them. Their vision is their soul statement. Values and core competencies are the vehicle and the fuel for corporate excellence in the future. Remember when it was the organizational structure, defined by the "org" chart and classified by titles and job responsibilities and the competence and talent of those who filled the boxes? Remember when you appraised a new prospect by the physical structure of the buildings and offices and work spaces they occupied, categorizing them by how lush and elegant or ergonomically arranged they were?

Not anymore! Now we have virtual corporations of team leaders in a mobile environment communicating through the Internet, Intranets, and groupware. What is the unifying structure? It is the CEO's vision. Your key to success is your ability to link your selling strategies to the CEO's goals. The door will open wider with every insightful and innovative idea or suggestion you offer that is aligned with the CEO's intentions.

Use every ounce of imagination and creativity you possess as you focus on your customer's business, seeking market opportunities and competitive advantages they are not even aware of. Use your special blend of talents to construct a solution that combines logic and emotion, analysis and creativity, the pertinent and the provocative.

Nolan Bushnell, founder of Atari and perpetual inventor and entrepreneur, calls this "skating on the visionary edge." Believing the step after the Information Age will be the Age of Creativity, he challenges us to dream up a concept that serves a customer so well, it changes people's lives.

Surge to the Next Level

Visionary Selling requires time. It requires work. I remember at one job when disgruntled salespeople would gather regularly in the parking lot to complain. The compensation plan was unfair and stifled our chances of earning a good income. Marketing was clueless, so out of touch with the customer that our marketing materials were a waste of paper and ink. Management—well, I can't even repeat what we said about them.

Although I tended to be a ringleader in these bitch fests, one year later I found myself in sales management. Now I was looking out my second-story office window to watch the clumps of complainers in the parking lot.

I'll bet your company has a "clump." Are you part of it? Abandon the clump. Just walk away. Invest the time instead in learning all about business. Track the trends. Investigate your customers and prospects to a deeper level of insight and innovation. Invest your awesome brainpower in improving their business.

If you accept my challenge, I offer a guarantee. You will enjoy the profession of sales to a degree you never dreamed possible. You will earn the respect, loyalty, and affection of your customers. You will increase your sales results and your compensation, whether or not your company's plan "sucks."

In the Chinese language, two written characters are often used to express one word. You are probably familiar with the Chinese depiction of the word crisis, which is composed of the symbols for danger and opportunity. The word for learning is a combination of the symbols for study and practice.

By reading this book you have completed the studying aspect of Visionary Selling. That is one-half of the total, but without the other it is of limited value. Take these ideas and practice them. Modify them when necessary to fit your environment or to adapt to your experiences.

The Thirty-Day Checklist

To improve any skill, the first step is an honest appraisal of where you are now. Assess where you stand today by checking each item on the following checklist that you are already using. When you begin researching a new prospect, record a date when each item will be completed.

__ Read *The Wall Street Journal* regularly.
__ Conduct extensive company research before initial contact.
__ Understand business concepts and terminology.
__ Approach the "C" level at business and social events.
__ Communicate frequently with top executives.
__ Enlist executives in your company in peer-to-peer selling.
__ Transform administrative assistants into allies.
__ Sell to decision makers that are on a higher level than those your peers sell to.
__ Share insightful information and provocative ideas.
__ Step into the role of "C" level counsel and "C" level catalyst.

Revolutionize the Profession of Sales

In *The Road Ahead,* Bill Gates states that "some middlemen who handle information or product distribution will find they no longer add value and change fields, whereas others will rise to the competitive challenge."

Rise to the competitive challenge! You will be creating the salesperson of the future. You will be participating in the mission of Visionary Selling: to revolutionize the profession of sales by simultaneously offering greater value to customers and greater purpose to salespeople.

Resources

Reading List

American Demographics
Business Ethics
Business Week
Common Cause
The Economist
Fast Company
Forbes
Fortune
The Futurist
Harvard Business Review
The National Times
The New Republic
Partisan Review
Policy Review
Sloan Management Review
The Wall Street Journal
Wired
Industry publications for their specific industry

Many of these publications are now available online, where you can quickly scan the information and select articles which are most relevant to you for in-depth study.

Glossary of Financial and Business Terms

Financial Terms

Acid test: The ratio of a company's liquid assets to short-term debts (also known as quick ratio).

Annual meeting: A stockholder meeting, normally held at the same time each year, to review the year's results and elect the board of directors.

Annual report: Yearly record of a corporation's financial condition that must be distributed to shareholders under Security and Exchange Commission (SEC) regulations. Included in the report is a description of the company's operations as well as its balance sheet and income statement. Usually available two or three months after the end of the fiscal year, it is a good source of information on the products and services of the company and on the company's management. The long version of the annual report with more detailed financial information is called the 10K. The quarterly report required by the SEC is a 10Q.

Balance sheet: A financial statement showing the company's assets on the left (what it owns) and the liabilities (what it owes) and the difference, called net worth or stockholders equity, on the right. The two sides are always in balance, since the net worth is the difference between assets and liabilities.

Board of directors: Group of individuals elected, usually at an annual meeting, by the shareholders of a corporation to carry out certain tasks as spelled out in the corporation's charter. They are empowered to appoint senior management, name members of executive and finance committees, issue additional shares of stock, and declare dividends. Boards normally include the top corporate executives, termed inside directors, as well as outside directors chosen from business and from the community at large to advise on strategy and policy.

Book value: The equity value of an outstanding share of stock, determined by dividing the amount of stockholders equity to which each share is entitled by the number of shares outstanding.

Budget: A forecast of revenue and expenditure for a forthcoming period for a part of a business.

Business cycle: Describes the expansion or contraction of the economy as a whole and has an important influence on the earnings of most companies. It contains eight key items:

1. Trends in consumer confidence and spending (book-to-bill ratio in high technology)
2. Actions by the Federal Reserve Board to tighten or ease the supply of money
3. Interest rate trends
4. The government's index of leading indicators
5. Tax increases or tax cuts
6. The accumulation or liquidation of business inventories
7. Capital expenditure plans of businesses for new plants and equipment
8. Government spending for defense and social needs.

Capital budget: Program for financing long-term outlays such as plant expansion, research and development, and advertising.

Capital expenditure: Outlay of money to acquire or improve assets such as buildings or machinery.

Capital formation: Creation or expansion of assets or of producer's goods through savings, resulting in economic expansion.

Capital gain: An increase in value realized on the sale or exchange of securities, fixed property, or similar assets.

Capital loss: A decrease in value realized on the sale or exchange of securities, fixed property, or similar assets.

Capital market: Source for long-term funds needed to expand existing businesses or start new ones. Primary: New money is raised from investors in the form of shares, bonds, or long-term bank loans. Secondary: Investors trade shares on the stock markets.

Capitalization: All money that has been invested in the business including equity capital (common stock and preferred stock), long-term debt (bonds), retained earnings, and other surplus funds.

Cash conversion cycle: Elapsed time from the outlay of cash for raw materials to the receipt of cash after the finished goods have been sold. This cycle is directly affected by production efficiency, credit policies, and other controllable factors.

Cash flow: A statement of the amount of ready money in a company during a specific time.

Chief executive officer/CEO: The highest-ranking corporate executive.

Chief financial officer/CFO: The highest-ranking company executive who handles its funds.

Chief information Officer/CIO: Responsible for implementing technology that will achieve the organization's goals.

Chief operating officer/COO: Usually the second-ranking corporate executive. Responsible for day-to-day management.

Cost accounting: The detailed itemization of the expenses connected with manufacturing a product or providing a service.

Cost-benefit analysis: A systematic process to measure the value of all the advantages that will accrue from a particular expenditure.

Current assets: Property owned that is expected to be converted to cash within one year.

Current liabilities: Obligations that will be paid within one year.

Current ratio: The relationship between current assets and current liabilities, calculated by dividing assets by liabilities. Having current assets that are at least twice current liabilities is considered a healthy financial condition.

Deficit: An excess of expenses over income.

Depreciation: The estimated decrease in value of property due to use, deterioration, or obsolescence over a period of time.

Dividend: A payment to stockholders, usually in the form of a quarterly check. It is declared by the board of directors and is normally determined by the level of the company's earnings.

Dow-Jones Industrial Average: A list of thirty major companies representing all industries whose prices are averaged daily to monitor market trends.

Earnings: The amount of profit a company realizes after all costs, expenses, and taxes have been paid. (Also called *net earnings.*)

Earnings per share: The profit divided by the average number of shares outstanding.

Going public: A term used to describe the sale of shares of a privately held company to the public for the first time. (Also called IPO or initial public offering.)

Gross profit margin: Net sales less the cost of goods sold.

Hurdle rate: The return required for the project to be worthwhile. The hurdle rate is crucial in making judgments about capital expenditure.

Income statement: A financial report that presents a company's business results (revenues, costs and expenses, taxes and earnings) over a specific period of time, usually quarterly or annually.

Interim report: A quarterly declaration of a company's income statement and sometimes the balance sheet. During the year, a company will issue three interim reports and one annual report.

Inventory turnover: Ratio of annual sales to inventory, which shows how many times the inventory of a firm is sold and replaced during an accounting period.

Leverage: The amount of debt in a company's capital structure; if the company is highly leveraged, its proportion of debt relative to equity is high.

Moving average: Average of security or commodity prices constructed on a period as short as a few days or as long as several years, showing trends for the latest interval.

Net earnings or net income or net profit: The amount a company realizes after all costs, expenses, and taxes have been paid.

Net profit margin: The profitability of a company after taxes are paid, calculated by dividing net earnings by total revenues.

Operating profit: The amount a company earns before taxes are paid.

Operating profit margin: The profitability of a company's operations before taxes are paid, calculated by dividing income received by sales.

Pretax margin: The profitability of a company before taxes are paid, calculated by dividing pretax profits by total revenues.

Pretax profits: The amount a company earns before paying taxes, determined by deducting all costs and expenses other than taxes from total sales.

Price earnings ratio or P/E ratio: The relationship between the cost of a stock and its earnings per share, calculated by dividing the stock price by the earnings-per-share figure.

Profit center: Segment of a business organization that is responsible for producing income on its own.

Profit margin: The profitability of a company measured by relating profits to revenues. The three most common profit margin calculations are operating profit margin, pretax profit margin, and net profit margin.

Quick ratio: See *Acid test.*

Retained earnings or earned surplus: Monies that have been reinvested in the business after or instead of dividends being paid to stockholders.

Return on equity: The amount a company earns on stockholders' equity, calculated by dividing net earnings by average stockholder's equity.

Shares authorized: The maximum number of stock portions allowed to be issued under a corporation's charter.

Shares outstanding: The number of authorized stock portions that have been issued and are now in the hands of owners.

Stockholder's equity: The difference between a company's total assets and total liabilities.

Working capital or net working capital: The excess of current assets over current liabilities.

Reengineering Terms

Benchmark: A standard determined by comparisons of results achieved by different organizations for a specific item, problem, or test.

Benchmarking: The process of determining a standard by which other items may be compared, measured, or judged.

Breakthrough performance: Unusual gains that are unreasonable to expect from a continuation of current management methods.

Business Process Reengineering (BPR): The rapid and radical redesign of strategic, value-added business processes—and the systems, policies, and organizational structures that support them—to optimize work flow and productivity in an organization.

Process: A series of interrelated activities that convert business inputs into business outputs.

Stakeholder: Anyone who has a vested interest in a process and in the outcome of reengineering the process.

Value-adding activities: Those actions that add value (from the customer's viewpoint) to the products or services produced by the process.

Vision: A high-level conceptualization of a desired result.

Management terms

Added value: The difference between what a company spends buying materials from outside and what it receives from selling its products, or the difference between a product or service sold for a specific price and the added value that the customer receives.

Business ecosystem: Companies working cooperatively and competitively to support new products, satisfy customers, and create the next round of innovation in key market segments.

Coevolution: The notion that by working with direct competitors, customers, and suppliers a company can create new businesses, markets, and industries.

Critical path method (CPM): A planning process used to determine how to complete a complex task in as short a time as possible.

Cycle time: The measured period allotted to each workstation on an assembly line to perform the assigned task for each unit.

Decision tree: A diagram that allows a decision maker to evaluate several alternative courses of action by assigning values to alternative outcomes.

Differentiation: Positioning a product or service as superior or different in relation to its competitors.

Downside risk: The worst possible outcome of a management decision.

Intrapreneurship: Promotion of the qualities of the entrepreneur inside a large corporation.

Market share: A company's sales in a particular product area expressed as a percentage of total sales in that area.

Matrix structure: A two-dimensional diagram showing management lines of responsibility both horizontally and vertically.

Opportunity cost: The expense resulting from not doing something.

Positioning: Defining a distinct set of characteristics that differentiate a product or service from its competitors.

Strategic intent: The broad long-term objective of a corporation; it also implies a point of view about the competitive position a company hopes to build over the coming decade.

Strategic IQ test: A fourteen-part questionnaire designed by Benjamin Tregoe and John Zimmerman to determine how strategy oriented a company is.

Stretch goals: A tangible corporate goal or destiny that represents a stretch for the organization, as described by Gary Hamel and C. K. Prahalad.

Value chain: The interlinking activities carried out within a corporation.

Value migration: The movement of growth and profit opportunities from one industry player to another.

Index

INDEX

INDEX

INDEX

INDEX

INDEX

About the Author

Barbara Geraghty is president of Idea Quest, a company that provides Visionary Selling keynote presentations and a unique sales training game, Klue. She speaks at national sales meetings, worldwide sales meetings, and association conventions to twenty-five thousand people annually. Her present clients include AT&T, Silicon Graphics, Sybase, and Siemens. She is a world traveler and a featured speaker on Crystal Cruises.

Barbara is a principal in IQ Accelerated Learning Systems, which provides a two-day education course, Visionary Selling to Executives.

Before founding Idea Quest in 1989, Barbara was a successful sales manager in Sprint's Pacific Division. She is a graduate of California State University, Fullerton, and is a member of the National Speakers Association. She lives in Irvine, California, with her husband and two daughters.

For more information about Visionary Selling, please visit our website at http://visionaryselling.com.